The
Loneliness
of the
Long Distance
Book
Runner

William Geraint Rees lives between Bangor and Montpellier, and makes his self-proclaimed 'precarious' living by translating French football matches into English for a Dutch bookmaker, as well as selling the occasional book. As a graduate of Bangor University, Rees worked as a reporter for a local newspaper in London, before the lure of travel and bookselling led him to take a less conventional road.

The
Loneliness
of the
Long Distance
Book
Runner

Bill Rees

PARTHIAN

Parthian
The Old Surgery
Napier Street
Cardigan
SA43 1ED

www.parthianbooks.com

First published in 2011
© Bill Rees 2011
All Rights Reserved

ISBN 978-1-906998-92-9

Editor: Lucy Llewellyn

Cover design by www.theundercard.co.uk
Typesetting by Lucy Llewellyn
Printed and bound by Gwasg Gomer, Llandysul

Published with the financial support of the Welsh Books Council.

'Mighty hunters of books encompass the earth, tracking down their quarry in all places, sacred and profane, monasteries and churches, castles and palaces; manor houses and rectories; flats, villas, cottages; shops of many kinds; town or country, it is all one, and the earth is all one to them as they cross the sea in swift liners, cover the land by train or automobile, and cleave the air in flying machines. Nor the does the hunting end at such personal contact as modern transport opens up to them; they hunt from wherever they are, throwing their nets over all lands by telephone, telegram, cable and radio, so that time and place and circumstances are annihilated in this sweet game, as in no other sport.'

The Anatomy of Bibliomania by Holbook Jackson.

Saint Pargoire, Southern France, 1995

Outside Alan Sillitoe's holiday home, I am loading my trusty Renault Express van with the author's donation of books and papers. A raised English voice pierces the incessant drone of cicadas and Alan Sillitoe rushes out into the sun-baked road. It turns out that I've inadvertently removed the wrong pile of books from the hallway. We check the boxes together to find that they contain precious first editions and personal manuscripts. I lug the boxes back and retrieve the items that were destined for me; obscure pamphlets by self-published poets and arcane miscellany.

The property is being sold, a fact relayed to me weeks earlier when I was introduced to the writer at a lunch hosted by a mutual acquaintance. He politely expresses an interest in my new venture – that of setting up a second-hand English bookshop in nearby Montpellier. He tells me that if he hadn't been able to write books, he would have wanted to sell them. And would I be interested in some free stock...

(Distance travelled: 74 miles. Profit: None. Fact learned: Enforced boredom gets the creative juices flowing. Well, it does the trick for Mr Sillitoe, he says.)

Inspecting Heirlooms in the Attic, Bangor, 2001

The lettering. And the colour. Off the page it hits with the promise of a revelation. Page 57 shows Bee at the controls of a crane being used to assemble Kind Dog's chunky cake. 'So on this day that was called Wednesday, Ant and Bee made Kind Dog a birthday cake out of dog biscuits, by sticking the biscuits together with sandwich filling. All day on that Wednesday Ant and Bee enjoyed making the birthday cake for Kind Dog.'

The picture and accompanying text of Ant and Bee first entered my head three decades ago. Now its recollection has a hallucinogenic quality. As do memories of early birthdays. Eddy and my mates came, most of them suited up like mini mobsters and drawn to the Real Sweet Stuff, which primarily took the form of a chocolate encrusted Thomas the Tank Engine bejewelled with smarties. Mum's signature cake.

The pages are still smudged with chocolate.

A Day's Pilgrimage to Hay-on-Wye, May 2008

Hay-on-Wye is the famous book town with its own literary festival described by Bill Clinton as the 'Woodstock of the mind.' With a surplus of paperbacks that need shifting, I intend to hit town several days before the literati arrive. I'd like to fill some of those minds with some of my books. So I go about filling up my Volks-book-battered-wagen with novels and petrol.

I leave Bangor in North Wales on a sunny day and intend to call on a few shops en route to Hay – a journey that will take me through the heart of Wales. I soon arrive at the gates of Caernarfon Castle and breach the town's medieval walls in order to call on a dealer specialising in mountaineering books. He's not averse to general fiction, but won't be buying today. He's in a hurry to get to some fair and only has the time to express his scepticism on the likelihood of selling books to the booksellers of Hay. Undeterred, I drive off and am uplifted by the gorgeous scenery. Around mountains and through forests, I wend my way to Dolgellau, a small market town situated at the foot of the Cader Idris mountain range in south Snowdonia. In the town is a charming bookshop whose owner still has an apparent market for cricket books. She buys a box of Huttons, Evans, and Boycotts mixed in with the occasional Wisden. It turns out that her son runs the Dyfi Valley bookshop in nearby Machynlleth. I recall having sold him a rare book on archery. The other bookshop in Machynlleth is called Coch-y-Bonddu Books (named after a Welsh dry fly) and they are international dealers in books on angling. They have bought specialist books on salmon fisheries from me, but I have nothing to tempt them today.

A red kite hovers at eye level while I drive along a pass before Machynlleth where I stop only for a late lunch. It's past mid-day and I must be wary of the distracting scenery. Grabbing a lamb oggie, I am soon back on the road, and an hour later, I am seeking out The Great Oak Bookshop in the streets of Llanidloes, a town with timber framed buildings. It's easily found but the owner expresses not the slightest bit of interest when I speak of a car full of books. No mention has been made of the prices and it amazes me that her interest hasn't been piqued.

I've been dawdling and I need to get a move on to arrive at Hay with enough time to call on potential buyers. The country roads lose some of their charm when you need to negotiate them at greater speed. On the outskirts of Hay, giant white marquees are going up in preparation for the festival. I'd like to take time in absorbing the atmosphere of the town that boasts thirty bookshops. But I don't have that luxury today. It's 4 p.m.; the shops are scheduled to close in one hour. In random fashion, I enter shops to speak of the book bonanza lying within my fourteen fruit and veg boxes. Several shop assistants are intrigued and follow me out to the car but most don't get that far. Their interest fades at the suggestion that I'm in the trade. Sure, they won't discover a first edition *Biggles*, but the stock is surely worthy of inspection. Several more shops can't commit because their buyer isn't in, and I'm beginning to get a little panicky at the thought of having to haul eight hundred books back through Wales this evening. There's only one thing to do; attack the castle.

Hay Castle Bookshop is situated in the public rooms and grounds of the castle, which overlooks the town. It is owned by Richard Booth, creator of the 'book town' concept and self-proclaimed King. Having briefly met him before (with the greeting of 'what do you flog then?') in Montolieu, a French version of Hay, I trudge up the steps to his abode and ask to see him. He's abroad, I'm informed by a lady at the till. A tactical decision not to volunteer any information about being in the trade pays dividends, for my description of a carload of literature elicits genuine enthusiasm. She calls to someone in the tower and I wait patiently as that someone slowly descends the spiral staircase. A suited gentleman with a distinguished air and walking stick then accompanies me to my car down several flights of outside steps.

I have strategically placed 'stronger' titles towards the top of the boxes. 'Very good,' is the gentleman's assessment following a brief rummage. He explains that I can drive up and park behind the castle, which is a relief. I unload the books before the lady on the till explains that she is not in a position to write a cheque. Only the accountant, who makes an appearance on Tuesdays, can do that. I quickly knock up an invoice, which she signs.

Unburdened, the Volkswagen whizzes me back to Bangor in no time.

(Distance travelled: 245 miles. Takings (promised): £150. Fact learned: 'To travel hopefully is a better thing than to arrive'.)

(Footnote: following weeks of 'payment is imminent' promises on the telephone, Mrs Booth phoned me to apologise for the 'mess' she and Richard had just returned to find. A cheque was then promptly sent.)

Emmaüs Near Calais, Late August 2007

Calais, overlooking the Strait of Dover, is the closest French town to England, just 21 miles away. For several centuries Calais was a British territorial possession. Nearby is an outpost of Emmaüs, the French equivalent to the UK charity shop. For many years they have been collecting and sorting all kinds of second-hand goods: clothes, electrical appliances, furniture, and of course books. Abbé Pierre founded the first Emmaüs community in the 1950s with a view to reducing social exclusion in society. Admirable sentiments, which do not, I'm afraid, account for my interest.

I intend to visit an Emmaüs warehouse near Calais and so investigate a developing theory, that over the years English books might have 'washed up' like driftwood in Calais, those left behind in hotels and on the ferries. Surely they would have a good chance of finishing up with Emmaüs.

Having kipped in the car, parked in a service station near Lille, I am feeling as dishevelled as I look. The previous day's 600-mile drive up through France has taken it out of me. I arrive early and wait for a café to open. There are groups of young men skulking down side streets. Such is my appearance, I could almost be mistaken for one of them. But these people are truly desperate; young men seeking food and dignity and attempting to complete the final leg of their journey to Britain. They are probably inhabitants of 'The Jungle', a collection of makeshift tents and cardboard structures which are home to hundreds of migrants, predominantly from the Middle East and Northern Africa. Even Emmaüs can't help these men, 'les sans papiers'.

A local reveals that the Calais branch of Emmaüs is not actually in Calais. It is in a village some seven miles south of the port called Attaques – a name to embolden the hunter-gatherer. At the appointed hour, 10.00 a.m., the shutters open and in we go. The usual suspects accompany me; people on the look out for antiques and resellable bric-a-brac. Inside the building there is plenty of the bric and the brac and, to be frank, the all round tat. A receptionist, bemused by my accent, directs me to the '*livres etrangers*' shelf. Musty smelling Penguins, unopened Orwells, a couple of Dicks (by which I mean Philip K.) and the ubiquitous *The Moon's a Balloon* by David Niven. It isn't the haul I'd been hoping for. But there is one hardback, sandwiched between two Bibles, that is a gem, though not in any financial sense. It is Holbrook Jackson's *The Anatomy of Bibliomania*. The first sentence reads:

> 'Books, the most excellent and noble creations of Man, are, saith one, for company, the best Friends; in doubts Counsellours; in Damps Comforters; Time's Prospective, the home Traveller's Ship, or Horse, the busie man's best Recreation, the Opiate of Idle Weariness, the Mindes best Ordinary, Nature's Garden and Seed-plot of Immortality.'

En Route to Llangollen, Wales, July 2009

Driving along the A5, the brooding, awful mountains are a fitting landscape for dark musings on the book business. I've recently closed down a shop; the venture culminated in a mega 'all books must go' sale. Books were given away, first figuratively such was their cheapness, and then literally, to passers-by and charity shops. During the cull, I pictured myself as a biblio-chemist, involved in some esoteric process of distillation. Book club editions and beach reads were jettisoned. I find that I'm left with an increased proportion of non-fiction titles that command a higher monetary value than most prose. I keep only the books that I perceive as food for the net. Aside from the occasional car boot sale, I'm now primarily a seller on the internet, of which I was an early enthusiast. But my view of it these days is more ambivalent. I can now sell a book to a customer hundreds of miles away. But the technology enabling me to do this is, of course, available to the customer, the middleman cut out.

The bookshop that I'm heading to in Llangollen, a town associated with the Eisteddfod and the River Dee, is a bit of an enigma. Above a greasy spoon café, a former chapel-like building now accommodates a large and incongruous stock. 'One hundred thousand books', proudly declared at the entrance to cafe. I spend hours traipsing the aisles, familiarising myself with the layout. There is a great deal of perusing done while a desultory trail of customers come and go. Most are looking for specific books. I, on the other hand, am taking in all the categories, trying to decide on what books are, from my perspective, underpriced.

It's soon clear that thousands of books here have no potential buyers. Dead authors and illustrators that have long since lost their allure. The observation is a salient reminder of a bookseller's ongoing fight against obscurity and, ultimately, extinction. There are exceptions of course. The shop's impressive collection of Penguin Classics is tangible testament that certain stories, ideas and philosophies live on. It's a struggle to guess which ones from the twenty-first century will survive. I reprimand myself and focus instead on money and how it is to be made.

The shop's seemingly permanent half price sale makes this possible. The large numbers of multiple copies reveal the previous owners' penchant for 'remainders'. Going on hunch and memory, I attempt to locate titles that are both out of print and desirable, the former not necessarily leading to the latter. Finally I spot several candidates. *Occasional Prose* by Flannery O'Connor and *Six Plays* by Soyinka at £1.50 a book. These can be resold near to the £10 mark on Amazon. I snap them all up. In the children's section I leave with a £3 copy of *Masquerade* by Kit Williams – worth five times that on abebooks. I might be tempted to read the O'Connor book, being a fan of her short stories. But I have to be aware of when my personal tastes influence 'business' decisions.

I spend £65 in total and return to Bangor to price and list the books on the net.

I should be able to triple the outlay in time. How much time exactly is anyone's guess, which is why the margins have to be so high.

I've made one mistake, seduced by the bulky seriousness of John Lloyd's *History of the Electrical, Electronic, Telecommunications and Plumbing Union*, which seemed good value at £6. It turns out that were plenty of copies going for less money on Amazon, some priced as low as you can get. One penny. It's become a significant trend, especially with paperbacks, to set them for sale at a single penny. In listing a book, software programs can automatically undercut all other copies of the same title. The result is an ineluctable slide in price, but some dealers are still able to turn a profit on the postage.

(Distance travelled: 100-mile return trip. Profit (projected): £295. Fact learned: Thomas the Tank Engine is alive and well and tooting in mid Wales.)

Barnardo's Charity Shop, Caernarfon, 2002

Falling into conversation with a volunteer on the till, I learn that he, a well-dressed pensioner, is an old camera enthusiast before he realises what brings me into the shop. He wastes little time in requesting an atlas that designates countries of the British Empire in pink. For some time, rifling through the bags of shop donations, he's been on the look out for one to give to a friend.

I dig out a nineteenth-century Bartholomew that fits the bill. A little research reveals that the pink colour is probably derived from the eighteenth-century atlases that used red after William of Orange ascended to the English throne. Incidentally, the French had atlases depicting British Empire countries in grey.

I drop the atlas off at the shop, saying I'll call later since the volunteer is serving customers. The following week I'm aghast to hear that the atlas has been given to BNP leader Nick Griffin. My disapproval obviously hits home. Griffin's relationship to the shop volunteer undergoes a demotion; from friend to acquaintance. The pensioner is also embarrassed at having no money on him.

I never return to collect payment.

Ham, Surrey, 1989

In attending this adult education course, I am introduced to the exacting world of antiquarian book description and classification. There is talk about paper marks, vellum, leather binding, gilt tooling, marbled papers. I check up on Roman numerals.

Our assignment is to find an old book and classify it. From the Mind charity shop in St Margarets I buy the following book for two pounds: *A Sentimental Journey Through France and Italy* by Laurence Sterne,

London: Longmans, Green, and Co. London, 1888. Decorative Cloth. Fine. Joseph Pennell (illustrator). First Thus. 8o. Decorative Cloth. 268 pp pale green cloth, gilt lettering on spine, original illustrated endpapers, lavishly illustrated by the authors with very nice vignettes and full page etchings, large fold-out map of their tricycle journey in imitation of Sterne's sentimental journey.

I'm convinced that this must be worth a bomb. Steve, the course lecturer, puts me right by explaining that age isn't synchronous with value.

A Sentimental Journey Through France and Italy is a novel by Laurence Sterne, published in 1768, just months before the author's death. Three years earlier, Sterne travelled through France and Italy, and after returning decided to provide a more subjective account of his experiences, one that emphasised the discussions of personal taste and morals. Prior travelogues had stressed classical learning and objective points of view. Maybe it is also the rambling style of Sterne that I find appealing; a subconscious selection of sorts, one presaging a desire to go walkabout in Europe.

Anthony Hall, Staines Road, Twickenham, 1987

It was in Anthony Hall's that I became truly infected. The shop specialises in Russian and East European Studies but such books bear no responsibility. It is in front of the small bookcase, crammed full with Penguin Modern Classics, that I am waylaid. For a lifetime, as it happens.

I am drawn to Penguin Modern Classics with a pale green livery. On their covers are specially commissioned illustrations, or paintings, as they say, by kind permission of the artist. Penguin no longer has a team of in-house designers, which may account for the reduced aesthetic appeal of the current Classics list.

Working as a reporter, I can keep unconventional office hours. At unshackled moments, I sneak into Anthony Hall's. In the course of several months, the shop's collection of Penguin Classics becomes my collection of Penguin Classics. I find myself making lists of books obtained and books wanted. I am lost. Skimming excitedly through the pages of the *Book Collector* magazine, I am in book list nirvana.

Fast forward twenty years to Bangor Bookshop where a customer tells me he got his diagnosis in the Hughes' Llandudno bookshop, its renowned and much respected owner declaring: 'You've got it bad, haven't you?'

Books, and dealing in them, get into your blood, but there is normally a collecting gene already there, whether it be for books, toy trains or airliner luggage labels.

Fez, Morocco, 1993

'Remember me. I can give you spices for your mind,' he says. Then he laughs, realising that I will not be sampling his wares. The purveyor of 'spices' is content to make conversation, commercially driven or otherwise. This is typical of the Moroccans I meet. A striving to sell, followed by a philosophical grin when their pitch fails to work.

The *Daily Awaaz*, a bilingual (Urdu and English) British daily newspaper based in Southall, is paying some of my expenses. I am tasked with returning with pictures of Moroccan tiles. They are to be immediately recognisable aspects of Moroccan art and architecture; zellij geometric mosaics first appearing in the late twelfth century in the city of Fez.

I have travelled from Casablanca. The great Hassan II Mosque is nearing completion but I haven't been able to properly approach it.

Mustapha clamours to capture my attention as I get off the coach in Fez. Fighting off rivals to win a coffee and vital time with a new tourist in town, he impresses me with his candour. 'You get hassle free time and I get money and a chance to practise my English,' went his line of patter. I explain to Mustapha the purpose, as it were, of my trip. He will help me take all the photos I need. Then, in producing a cigarette from nowhere, he sighs and proudly declares it to be his first of the day. It is Ramadhan and the day's fast is over. His mood is one of contentment and he is not alone. The wide streets of Ville Nouvelle are filling with people at ease. Family members stroll in relaxed fashion, arm in arm. Teenagers crack jokes. Small children skip with a spontaneous joy. As in Casablanca, most women are unveiled and clad in Western dress. Boys and teenagers tend to wear jeans whereas the men favour Djellaba cloaks.

It seems that the city of Fez still lingers in the Middle Ages. As you arrive in the city and begin to walk around your senses are torn between beautiful Islamic architecture, distressing poverty, alien sounds and an array of smells. And oranges, oranges galore. To the first time visitor, the two most obvious sources of income appear to be tourism and drugs. My guidebook sternly warns of the risks involved in smoking cannabis, in spite of the air being filled with its all-pervasive sweet aroma. Mustapha confirms, however, the danger inherent in smoking. 'Lots of arrests. Even for people like me.' Later he talks of an unexpected benefit following the police clampdown; a marked improvement in the quality of the drug.

Towards midnight I feel a chill in the air, but this does not deter devout Muslim men from staying up all night in the cafés, playing cards and smoking, thus ensuring that everyone will know that they have abstained from sex. Over coffee, we chat late into the night. Mustapha is keen to know what I do. I explain that in addition to working for a newspaper, I buy and sell books.

The next day is a whirlwind tour of the medina, and meeting the challenge of locating, through a maze of narrow streets, the sites of famous mosques. I take plenty of photos and think my editor will be happy with them. We gaze up at the minarets and listen to the strident sound of Islam calling the population to prayer. Seven veiled women and an infant are waiting patiently outside a mosque. Having just prayed, the men exit in a charitable frame of mind. The girl gratefully receives their donations, beaming with satisfaction, though her demeanour alters when approached by a man in a green uniform. All money is removed from her begging hand and redistributed among the waiting women. The girl is confused and starts to sob.

In the afternoon it rains and the medina is soon a mass of people engaged in noisy commerce. We do our best to avoid stepping in the thickening mud and donkey shit. Enterprising kids start selling plastic bags as makeshift coats to desperate sightseers.

After a conventional tour of the Imperial City, my clandestine guide directs me towards the Kasbah. The site of an old French fort is not mentioned in the guide book. Upon arriving, I see why. Only the castle walls remain and inside you come face to face with its inhabitants, who evidently live in grinding poverty. The ruins contain a shanty town where mothers hurry to remove their washing from makeshift lines. The faces of children peer out of corrugated huts. Mustapha tells me this is where his formative years were spent.

The rain is falling more heavily and young women exit the Kasbah with care to prevent the mud from splattering their smart costumes. A dignified and neat appearance is at all times retained as family and friends embrace before breaking their fast as tradition demands. An atmosphere of wellbeing is once more settling upon the city of Fez as its inhabitants dine on spicy bean soup and egg. Afterwards, there are sweets and dates. At this time of the day and year, hospitality becomes an obligatory virtue. Several families invite me into their homes to eat simple but tasty meals. A friend of Mustapha learns of my interest in football and informs me of a game scheduled for tomorrow.

Not being a fan, Mustapha isn't pleased about attending a football match. I don't force him to watch but he feels obliged to keep me company, concerned by the possibility of other guides encroaching upon his territory – me. Palm trees encircle the stadium, which is by no means full, but there is a good atmosphere. We take our seats next to men who wear tasselled hats. Music starts and the tassels are swirled about. The business of fasting is taken seriously, even sportsmen are not exempt. (Reassuringly, airline pilots do not observe the fast.) Despite the fast both teams play with energetic abandon. Mas, the home side, perform with admirable skill and determination. Their win against RAJA, one of Casablanca's top clubs, is made sweeter still by it ensuring the club's survival in the top flight. The home supporters celebrate by dancing jigs of victory.

The medina of Fez is believed to be the world's largest car-free urban area. The market inside is a treasure hunter's labyrinth of leather goods, carpets, brass work, silver, gold and the world's finest hashish, so Mustapha claims. We venture deeper into the medina. Mustapha says we should visit a Riad, a traditional Moroccan house. In a lane adjacent to the main thoroughfare of Fez's medieval quarter, the door is already open. Mustapha nods to a young man slouched outside. We step inside. The house is built on several levels around an interior garden that boasts a solitary orange tree. The ground floor appears sparsely furnished and there is a simple kitchen. We ascend a few stairs and Mustapha can't resist showing me the bathroom that is covered floor-to-ceiling in zellij mosaic tiles. I already have enough photographs of them. And Mustapha gestures that he has brought me here for other reasons. A little further up the stairs we come to more rooms on the first and second floors. He shows off the cedar ceilings, windows and doors, and the carved tadelakt plasterwork. I have read that these houses were inwardly focused to allow for family privacy and protection from the weather. But where is the family? Away, Mustapha simply says. And then he takes me into a room that is magnificently furnished with books. 'You buy,' explains Mustapha. 'I sell for professor friend.' The books are mostly in French and Arabic. I spot some Flaubert and I recognise some that are translations of Paul Bowles' novels. *Un thé au Sahara* is a French edition of *The Sheltering Sky*, which I have in my hotel room. Gore Vidal cites the book as one of his favourites. Think, he says, about what Bowles means by the 'sheltering sky' – that the 'sky' is a fiction, protecting us from our very insignificance. Mustapha is haphazardly picking out books for inspection; stories written by *'les ecrivains anglo-saxons'*. Thrilled by finding a book in English – an Edward Heath autobiography – he can't understand why I don't share in his excitement. But suddenly I am intrigued by an old looking edition of *Les Fleurs du Mal*. It has an 1861 publication date, which means that it was issued in Baudelaire's lifetime. (The second edition contains thirty-five additional poems but lacks six poems that appeared in the first edition. These were banned and stayed so until 1947.)

L'invitation au voyage
Mon enfant, ma soeur,
Songe à la douceur
D'aller là-bas vivre ensemble!
Aimer à loisir,
Aimer et mourir
Au pays qui te ressemble!
Les soleils mouillés
De ces ciels brouillés
Pour mon esprit ont les charmes

Si mystérieux
De tes traîtres yeux,
Brillant à travers leurs larmes.

Là, tout n'est qu'ordre et beauté,
Luxe, calme et volupté.

This book might be worth thousands of francs. How much does the owner want for it? Mustapha unhesitatingly says 5000 dirhams. That's about £400. I start to feel uncomfortable. It dawns on me that we may be trespassing. The price drops to 40 dirhams. The book's wildly fluctuating price confirms my fears. I hurriedly make my way down the stairs and exit the house. On the street outside, Mustapha is aggrieved. My hasty departure has been misinterpreted as an underhand negotiating ploy.

Montpellier Football Club Car Park, 1993

Traders buy and sell. Book dealers are no different. Books are bought and sold. Simply that. Open air markets appeal; their ancient and overt purpose of bringing buyer and seller together. Their 'openness' extends, somehow, beyond that of the physical selling arena. Not that I wish to romanticise; people can just as easily be ripped off here – openly or otherwise – as in other environments.

On Sunday mornings the car park adjacent to the city's football club comes to life as hundreds of car booters and professional traders join together to form a huge flea market known in French as *Les Puces*.

Such is *Les Puces* popularity with buyers and sellers alike, we arrive pre-dawn in order to guarantee a place in which to sell our wares – *livres en anglais*. Pulling up behind a Peugeot 807 fully packed with Indian jewellery and trinkets, we are struggling to come to terms with the early hour. The plan had been to snooze awhile but our growing anticipation, together with the activity of others outside, makes relaxation impossible. A hoard of bargain hunters shine torches into the back windows of the van but we make it clear that we're not yet open for business. We heed a friend's advice not to set up too soon. Jemal teaches geography in a local secondary school and supplements his salary by selling Moroccan pottery he transports from his home village in the long summer break. He warns that certain traders/hustlers will pounce, like the proverbial early bird, on the items brought to the market by unwary families, which are then brazenly sold on later that same morning from their own stalls.

We grab coffee, experience the early morning chill. We then take a tour as the rising sun reveals the sheer variety of goods on offer. Plenty of clothes and bric-a-brac along with an eclectic mix of junk and antiques. The place is lent an exotic flavour by the rugs from North Africa, Rai music blaring out. All classes of society will soon be caught up in the age-old customs of surveying and scrutinising. In catching the mood of the market, we adopt an easy stroll while casting a keen eye. By observing some of the early transactions I ascertain that haggling is very much de rigour.

In spite of the variety of stalls and merchandise about, it is still with a slightly embarrassed air that we set up, unfolding the pasting table upon which the books, mostly paperbacks, are laid out. To my relief, nobody bats an eyelid. The books are casually surveyed. A few people linger to take in the titles and only one elderly gentleman chooses to express surprise over their language. In opening a shop one year later, I am met with considerably more scepticism from passers by. One guy even insinuates that the shop must be some kind of front for ill-gotten gains. I try to look affronted but take perverse pleasure from the thought.

Our spirits receive an early boost when a man, with dishevelled hair that gives him a somewhat professorial air, snaps up our entire collection of Sotheby's Art Auction catalogues. Great. We're in profit.

Although it's only nine in the morning the alleys are thronging with punters. As the sun rises higher, we understand the advantage of being in the row of cars opposite us, for they lend the sellers a modicum of shade. We are forced to beat a retreat into the van and cast envious glances at people who erect makeshift awnings. The covers of some books curl under the fierce sun and there are sporadic gusts of winds that have me reaching for elastic bands to stop the pages from being blown about. Conversations are started with neighbours and an inchoate camaraderie means that we mind each other's stands to permit toilet breaks and 'getaway' tours of the market when boredom thresholds are reached.

'Ah, *Travels in the Hindu Kush*. I've been there,' a Dutch holidaymaker informs us. 'Buy it to remind yourself of the experience,' I reply as he leafs through it. I fail to convey the intended humour for he takes seriously my comment. 'You really can't compare the two. You need to go.' He returns the book to the table before buying a couple of Agatha Christies whose gaudy covers attract the attention of many browsers.

In taking a distinctly scenic route back from a declared 'coffee and croissants top up mission'. I scan some of the stalls and spot a 1884 edition of *Pall Mall Magazine*. I note that Father Christmas is depicted in what we, these days, assume is his traditional garb; a bulky red coat with white trims to go with a large white beard. I'd thought that the look had come later, derived from Coca-Cola ads. This makes me buy the magazine for 10 francs and I am later pleased to discover that it has in it 'Aepyornis Island', a short story published for the first time by HG Wells. It also has *Letting in the Jungle* by Rudyard Kipling, illustrated with a demonic looking Bagheera and Mowgli pictured as a naked Aryran child with a rather pert bottom. It's not what you might expect from the Victorians. Or maybe it is.

I return to our stall where a middle aged couple are intensely inspecting the books, many of which are now crammed together in boxes, with their spines facing out, so as to avoid the ravages of the sun. I hear snippets of their conversation, which is in English, and I soon gather that it is Ian McEwan and his wife. Living in France, the author has recently published *Black Dogs*, which is partly set in the Cevennes whose foothills are 40 miles to the north of Montpellier. The book is concerned with the lives of June and Bernard Tremaine that epitomise the tug-of-war between political engagement and a private search for ultimate meaning. The catalytic event in the Tremaines' lives occurs on their honeymoon in France in 1946. In an encounter with two huge, ferocious dogs – incarnations of the savagely irrational eruptions that recur throughout history – she has an insight that illuminates for her the possibility of redemption. A novel of ideas with the hard edge of a thriller; highly recommended. I have a first edition of this book at home in addition to a paperback of McEwan's first collection of short stories. I'm quite a fan and let him know. He offers to sign my copy but I haven't got it with me. (I go through phases of separating my private library of books from those to be flogged off.)

His wife, seeming to take umbrage at her husband's fame, wanders away and Ian McEwan decides finally to buy a couple of Henry James Penguins, one of which has been recently recommended to him. I later recount the story to a much valued customer in my bookshop who, it turns out, was a friend of McEwan when they both taught English as a foreign language in East Anglia.

(Distance travelled: 2 miles. Takings: 870 francs (courtesy of one Dutchman, four Frenchwomen and nine English people, including a famous writer). Fact learned: Markets are about endurance and chance encounters.)

Household Waste Recycling Centre, Llandegai, November 2007

I look into what is essentially a giant paper-compressing skip. What am I doing here with this family heirloom, a complete set of *Encyclopaedia Britannica* published in 1911? The pages are still legible inside heavily disintegrating red covers. But the CD Rom and more modern editions have made mine moribund, it seems. The charity shops reject such volumes. I can't give them away.

Taid, as a student at Manchester University, bought the set second-hand in 1919. He'd been invalided out of the front line trenches in the First World War not with war wounds but with severe goitre, which was subsequently treated with success by an early form of radium irradiation. From a modest background, Taid had made his purchase – which I think of as being the equivalent these days to a top of the range Apple Mac – with funds from the Government. He'd applied successfully for a Kitchener Scholarship, a grant given to those who fought in the war. It enabled him to enter higher education; he even professed never to have been so well off before or after his time as a student.

I do the deed before learning several months later that the *Encyclopaedia Britannica* 11th edition, 1911, is considered to be one of the most collectable. Damn. I discover further that it is a much sought after edition; the first to be published as a whole set at one date. It is seen as the most scholarly edition, with contributions by over one thousand authors writing in their fields of expertise. All have an abundance of illustrations including numerous foldout maps in both colour and black and white.

I confess to my ignorance and this act of vandalism.

Sunday Morning, Sète, 1997

We have come to the sea to taste tielle – a small spicy pie of octopus in tomato sauce – and show the children the water jousting tournaments in Sète harbour. Since the beginning of Sète, the men have practised a spectacular type of combat, which has been passed on through the centuries: jousts. Standing firm on their plank with the bowsprit overhanging the boat with its team of oarsmen, these knights, as they are called all along the banks of the Etang de Thau, brave one another with only a wooden shield and lance for protection. The tip of each lance is fitted with a triple steel point. The aim of the competition is to knock one's rival into the water.

The spectacle is yet to begin so I can't resist a 'really quick, I promise' visit to Sète's *Les Puces*, a scaled down version of Montpellier's complete with the North African influence. The family is keen to return to the harbour so I can't mess about. In jumping from car to car, I pick out some tatty green Penguins – crime titles – in a pile of mostly French books dumped in a higgledy piggledy fashion beside an equally disordered pile of clothing, much of which will be discarded when the market closes at midday. In rummaging about, a red hardback by P.G. Woodhouse, lacking its dust jacket, comes to the surface. *Love Among the Chickens*, 11th printing. It's in a pretty parlous state but my enthusiasm is rekindled when I open it to find an inscription on the title page: *To Joseph Wilkels in memory of a delightful two months at the Picardy. P.G. Wodehouse Sept 10 1934* referring to his stay at The Royal Picardy – Le Touuet-Paris Plage.

This will sell it.

Built upon and around Mont St Clair, Sète is situated on the south-eastern hub of the Bassin de Thau, an enclosed salt water lake used primarily for oyster and mussel fields. To its other side lies the Mediterranean. We eat some of its food after the 'jousting' entertainment. Before leaving Sète, we visit Cimetière le Py and find the tombstones of Georges Brassens, singer and songwriter, and Paul Valéry. Best known as a poet, Valéry is sometimes considered to be the last of the French symbolists. Anne tells me about 'Le Cimetière marin', a poem based on Valéry's musings by the Mediterranean where he spent his boyhood.

Ce toit tranquille, où marchent des colombes,
Entre les pins palpite, entre les tombes;
Midi le juste y compose de feux
La mer, la mer, toujours recommencée
O récompense après une pensée
Qu'un long regard sur le calme des dieux!

This quiet roof, where dove-sails saunter by,
Between the pines, the tombs, throbs visibly.
Impartial noon patterns the sea in flame –
That sea forever starting and re-starting.
When thought has had its hour, oh how rewarding
Are the long vistas of celestial calm!

(Distance travelled: 70-mile return trip. Profit (two years later): 1350 francs, sold through abebooks.com on account of Wodehouse's inscription. Fact learned: Business can be mixed with pleasure, sometimes.)

Decision Time, Twickenham Bedsit, 1989

A single duvet on a double bed. It means that Jennifer has left. Eddy sees this but averts his gaze out of a nebulous notion of decency. Partly to put distance between us and so mitigate the mutual discomfort, I am making coffee in the kitchen area. The relationship has partly defined me for almost six years: we do, we don't, we will, we won't. It is going to be a testing time; reacquainting myself with the personal pronoun.

Avoiding eye contact by concentrating my efforts on not spilling the coffee, I hand Eddy a cup with an air of exaggerated calmness. There is a flurry of words about resignations and a change of scenes. Excited by the prospect of leaving it all for Paris, I, too, become garrulous. Coach timetables are scrutinised as the hypothetical seemingly turns to something more substantial. Little attention is given to the television which is left on so as to provide background noise should conversation dry up. But there is little chance of that happening while grandiose plans of book dealing and travel are being made and, to some extent, made up. Getting carried away, he almost misses the last bus back home. It's nice of Eddy to have called. Our friendship has history and form.

We used to catch a bus and then the tube out to Heathrow Airport, ostensibly to watch planes. What we mostly did was wander Terminal 2, covertly helping ourselves to a panoply of baggage labels as well as anything else such as key rings and badges – all items offered by the airlines to passengers as freebies, which was how we also viewed them. Our Heathrow jaunts were considered self-made teenage entertainment in the late seventies; a successful Saturday afternoon culminating in a bag chock-full of tangled, multi-coloured paper that spoke of exotic destinations. Eddy was stopped on one occasion. I'd done a runner, leaving him to his fate. On the bus home, he relates the 'bollocking' that he'd been forced to endure.

Corcoran Irish Pub in Paris, 1990

Eddy has tipped me off. A Virginia Woolf? I don't seek out the pub immediately, deferring an anticipated pleasure. I walk in desultorily fashion until Corcoran's catches my eye. It is strange to walk off a French street and into an Irish pub. Irish by name but certainly not exclusively Irish by its patronage – inside is a mix of Brits and Parisians. Ireland is a country loved by the French; English boozers not commanding in gallic hearts anywhere near the same degree of romantic reverence. It can't really be a Celtic thing either; the continent is hardly overrun with Welsh or Scottish pubs. Maybe it's the Guinness label and their pure marketing genius.

The bar staff are unfailingly polite, graduates, perhaps, of a Guinness finishing school that produces clean-cut personable young men. In addition to pulling pints, they provide a social service for tourists and the homesick. This evening, I don't class myself as either. I'm here for business.

I order a pint and sit down in the corner to the right of the pub's door. This is where Eddy says he saw the book. The décor is typical: plenty of old pictures, mirrors, bric-a-brac, frames of old Guinness bottle labels and books to which I am drawn. There is a row of books on a single shelf running above my head. A frisson of excitement. Always the same. It's not just the thought of finding a valuable book. It's curiosity's pull. Corcoran's library comprises mostly small hardbacks lacking dust jackets.

Sipping Guinness, I survey the books whose spines have faded into a uniform appearance of greying grubbiness. On closer examination, beneath the dust, are the distinct hues of brown, green, red and blue. Book club editions, some with Boots Booklovers' Library labels. George Eliot's *Romola* in BCA plonked beside *Board of Traffic Offences*, third supplement to the 15th edition. And there, as Eddy has said, is a copy of *To the Lighthouse* by Virginia Woolf.

Taking care not to dislodge the surrounding titles, I reach

up and extract it from the shelf. There is no dust jacket but it is a first, the book published by The Hogarth Press in 1927. I wipe the dust off the blue cloth, revealing gilt title lettering on the spine. There are no inscriptions. People still aren't paying me any notice while I casually reach up to replace the book. Sipping more Guinness, I try to gather my thoughts.

A simple offer to buy it might raise suspicion. The thought to pocket it does cross my mind. Who would miss it? These books are for just for show, aren't they? I could try to justify the theft but I can't bring myself to actually steal a book. It feels wrong; it being a betrayal, as it were, of my trade. My moral compass, in spite of its innate dodginess, draws a distinction between a book and, say, a Cadbury cream egg whisked surreptitiously into a young boy's pocket. What to do? Maybe I should come clean and offer to go halves with the pub on any profit accrued from its future sale. I finish my pint and leave with the intention of returning tomorrow with a canny plan.

I don't need one.

Eddy has anticipated my prevarication. The following day in the Montparnasse McDonald's, over a greedily consumed McBacon roll, the book is plonked down before me. He'd simply asked Simon, one of the bar staff with whom he is on friendly terms, to take home the book. As easy as you like.

It has a firm binding with no leaning to its spine, which is unusual given its previous resting spot. The book contents are in very good condition; no spotting or any marks. I get lucky in London. A dealer in Virginia Woolf pays over the odds because he has an authentic dust jacket lacking its book. Being a highly sought after title, its sale generates a good deal of wonga which I happily share with Eddy. A good proportion of his share will be spent on beer... in Corcoran's.

Car Boot Sale at Mona, Anglesey, 2004

The sun is shining for once and it's great to be tramping about this windswept green field in Wales. We arrive late and so have the excuse to lunch on local lamb burgers washed down with tea. Emily is eating candyfloss and Matty is absorbed in adding to his collection of Disney films. Making the most of this small window of pester free time, I look through a box of history books. I also notice some Enid Blytons and an Oxenham. None of them have dust jackets but the lady selling them says that she only wants £15 for the lot. Fair enough.

Later that afternoon, with the help of the internet and some reference books, it becomes clear that the Oxenham, despite its less than pristine state, is highly collectable. There isn't another copy for sale on any of the main book websites.

After further deliberation and research, I upload the following details to my list of books in cyberspace.

Author: Elsie Oxenham
Title: Finding her family
Illustrator: W.S. Stacey
Publisher/ The Sheldon Press
some spotting to page edges, darkening to green cloth cover, picture on cover of girl on bed being consoled by a woman. Frontispiece of woman gazing out into garden, very rare book hence price £480

The book sells four months later and I try to justify my profit. How many car boots have I visited in order to find this gem of a collector's item?

The buyer in Australia might be a seller or a collector. I

have no way of knowing. She may well intend to sell the book on, providing that she has a customer or a better judgement of the book's value. A hierarchy of knowledge, the fundamental setter of price, determines the chain of book transactions.

(Distance travelled: 15 miles. Profit: £465. Fact learned: My business success is as unpredictable as Anglesey's weather.)

Tuesday Morning, Montpellier Auction, 1996

The room is packed with objects and people milling about them. I am slightly apprehensive. This is my first auction and I'm late which means there is only time for a cursory glance at the various lots. Beneath a settee, there is a box of books, which I crouch down to assess. There are plenty of Folio paperback classics and I consider them worth a bid. I've got increasing confidence in my judgement of French books.

The auction soon starts and the auctioneer is rattling through the bids. His voice lulls me into a trance-like state out of which I am jolted upon hearing the words '*boite du livres*'. I thrust my hand skywards and soon discover that nobody else wants to bid. Sixty francs is all I've offered and I feel slightly exhilarated to have participated and triumphed at my first attempt.

Successful bidders are expected to assemble fairly promptly at a desk near the hall's entrance where payment is made. In handing over the money, I am then puzzled when the auction 'ushers' walk straight past the box of books. They go instead to a massive mahogany headboard, which they need two men to carry. My mistake dawns on me.

'*Bois du lit*'. Idiot. Attempting to appear unfazed, I lead the assistants outside to my van into which they heave the bed. I feign contentment with my purchase until I drive out of their sight whereupon I unleash a volley of expletives.

(Distance travelled: 3 miles. Profit: None. Fact learned: A little knowledge in French can lead easily to humiliation.)

Southport, July 2009

Drawn to this smart town with a reputation for good bookshops, I am not disappointed. The owners at Kernaghan Books, situated in Wayfarers Arcade, are friendly and much of their stock is reasonably priced (by my definition) in that it can be bought and sold on. I willingly part with £10 to own the works of Voltaire and the diary of Jules Renard in the Bibliotheque de la Pleiade.

My next port of call is Broadhursts, established in 1926. The shop covers four floors and is a delight for any bookworm or bibliophile. Some of the rooms have a museum feel about them and they get me thinking. Broadhursts boasts an impressive array of *Biggles* and *Just Williams*. Many other books – including modern firsts – are struggling to fetch prices achieved in previous decades. W. E. Johns and Richmal Crompton have resisted this trend but for how long? The rule of supply and demand dictates but demand has no inherent hold on stability at the best of times. Collectors covet certain books because other collectors have previously done so and are continuing to do so. Someone is buying a book whose 'value' is based upon other people's assessment of its monetary worth. A philosopher acquaintance and former customer points out that these books as an investment are dependent on a third party's investment decision. He has me scratching my head and wading through Keynesian theories of economics in the tertiary sector.

Opening Bangor Bookshop, April 2007

The city is roofed in local slate – Penrhyn purple – which imbibes somehow the grey skies, something of a meteorological default setting in North Wales. To compensate, there is the timeless melancholic beauty of the mountains.

Bangor is really a small town although its compact cathedral confers upon it official city status. It has an old university (by today's standards) and a proud, friendly working class community. There is an absence of snobbishness but Bangor is still, in other respects, a microcosm of Britain, and somewhat schizoid in nature; PhD meeting KFC: professors intoxicated by the abstruse, lads on lager overload, seaweed from Japan for sale in Upper Bangor's health food shop while, below, the city's High Street is awash with the country's regulation fare. Seagulls gorge on the leftovers. A plethora of chippies but no fishmonger. Packed pubs at weekends. Drunk students, skunked students, but studious ones too, that, I hope, will buy second-hand books. Some locals resent their presence and the mess of their rubbish spilling out of discarded bin liners. But they are the lifeblood of the city, and in the High Street, at the cheapest end, I open a bookshop prosaically called 'Bangor Bookshop'.

I make a stab at targeting the university market but the margin on academic texts is, after a student discount, fifteen per cent at best. It makes more sense to concentrate on used books. Rents and rates mean that I have to conjure, from book sales, some £800 a month before I've made a penny. I'm struggling from the start.

The truth of it is that not enough people buy my books. Unhesitatingly, the public buys newspapers and magazines. But not books. Arnold Bennett in the 1920s announced that he had 'scarcely ever met a soul, who could be said to make a habit of buying new books. Most people look upon money spent upon books as money wasted: the public hates to spend money on books, although they do not hesitate to spend lavishly on such ephemera as newspapers and magazines.' *Plus ça change...*

A pub opposite, The White Harp, makes me think if only people could get drunk on books, ordering one after another. Hey, this Rankin is the business, bookseller, serve me up another three more Rebuses and a Dexter chaser.

Rogers Jones Auction House, Colwyn Bay, March 2003

On the 'viewing' eve of the monthly antiques sale in Colwyn Bay, an oak Welsh dresser distracts me from the purpose of our visit. Anne gets me back on track by spotting *The Speaking Picture Book for the amusement of Children by Image, Verse and Sound*.

Lot 278 intrigues. The pages are inside a carved wooden

box upon which is a colour pictorial label. At the front of the book are eight fine chromolithograph illustrations, each facing a page of text. Next to each page of text is an ivory knob that, when gently pulled, causes a different animal sound to be produced (cock, donkey, lamb, birds, cow, cuckoo, goat and mamma and papa).

I've never seen anything like it. It's a half book half toy antiquarian oddity. We return home and the internet sets my pulse racing. Haining (*Moveable Books*, p. 136–7) calls this 'the piece de resistance of any collection of moveables' and adds that few complete and fine copies have 'survived youthful hands'. The guide price in the auction catalogue is £250–£300 which is well out of kilter with valuations on various websites. There are copies going on abebooks.com for well in excess of £1000.

I rush back to Colwyn Bay to convince myself that it is the book that was published in Sonneberg, Germany by Theodor Brand in 1880. All evidence indicates that it is. The label on the cover notes that this is 'A new picture book'. Inside the front cover is a printed label at the bottom of which reads 'A German edition is also appearing.' It also notes that it is patented in Great Britain, the United States, Germany and Austria. The thought of a patented book appeals to me.

The next morning in the salesroom I wait nervously for Lot number 278. I have my card at the ready. On arrival you register your details at reception and they provide you with a bidding number on a card. This is what you raise to the auctioneer's attention when you want to place bids.

Wondrous items abound but I'm transfixed by the possibility of owning *The Speaking Picture Book*. The auction is in full swing. The salesroom is heaving. Rogers Jones' employees hold phones to their ears; their faces tensed up with concentration. They bid on behalf of what I imagine to be wealthy dealers in locations rather more exotic than Colwyn Bay. It creates a buzz of excitement. Prices rocket. The gavel is thumped down with theatrical glee.

We are up to Lot 30 when a couple of middle aged men push down to near the front where I anxiously stand. Almost immediately one of them begins to bid with reckless extravagance, or so it seems to me. Spending thousands of pounds on furniture, jewellery and old grandfather clocks, his budget seems limitless. He wasn't at yesterday's evening 'viewing'. In his hand is an unblemished catalogue, with nothing scribbled down in the way of notes and prices. I get the impression that he is in the business of making instantaneous assessments. Lot 278, by chance, is displayed on a table within three metres of us. Minutes before the auctioneer comes to it, the Big Spender steps up to give it the once over. The 'viewing period' is clearly over but the auctioneer tolerates this minor disregard for convention.

As with most of the items, the auctioneer talks up the book in his pre-bid spiel. And suddenly, we're off. 'Let's start at £250.' Nobody bats an eyelid and the price drops to £80 before anyone will offer a starting bid. It is me. Two other people also express interest and the bidding reaches £210 before they drop out. My heart beats hard. The auctioneer is appealing for more bids. 'This seems cheap to me. Going...' Damn. The Big Spender lifts up his card. The bidding advances in £10 intervals. Trying to out bluff my competitor, I hold the card aloft, not bothering to bring it down after my bid. But he does the same. The price races to £350, my top bid figure or so I'd thought. Breaking this promise to myself, I go to £420 before conceding defeat.

The auction ends and the Big Spender is swigging from a can of Coke while counting cash with his colleague. Strangely, I feel like congratulating him. I want to tell him about the book's history but all I say in parting is 'That's a nice book.'

'Aye,' he replies in a thick Glaswegian brogue. 'I just liked the look of it.'

(Distance travelled: 40 miles. Profit: None. Fact learned: Knowledge is power, but it can be trumped by big money.)

Four Months Later, Another Auction in Colwyn Bay

This isn't the antiques sale, rather the general household. They've made a mistake. Intensive rummaging of four boxes of mixed books has produced nothing but dust and disappointment. But then I come across Lot 56, assigned to a box of old children's books, most of which are in a sad state of disrepair. Amongst these and in fairly good condition is the classic *The Square Book of Animals* by William Nicholson. It is what it says. It has a marvellous symmetry about it, even its publication date – 1900. It is a picture book of British animals explained in rhymes by Arthur Waugh. A £15 bid allows me to leave with the box and all the books therein.

Later that evening, I type up the following description: *William Heinemann 1900, First Edition Boards VG Some shelf wear and corner wear. Complete with 12 plates by Nicholson. Offsetting of plates to facing text pages, otherwise, clean. Two plates with a small brown spot in margin.*

In 1897 Nicholson made a woodcut of Queen Victoria which established his name with the public. During the same year he worked upon *An Illustrated Alphabet* for the publisher William Heinemann. It was reasonably successful commercially, but more importantly, it provided Nicholson with an opportunity to develop his talents as an engraver. There is something immensely appealing about his work. I'd like to keep *The Square Book of Animals* but my finances preclude ownership. It reminds me of the format of my first alphabet books. John Burningham's *ABC* with an apple, birds, etc., through to xylophone, yacht and zoo. One letter on each page is shown in both upper and lower case, along with a relevant word. On the facing page is a simple illustration in pastel colours. *The Square Book of Animals* is an ancestral version of the format.

Its appeal is widespread. It soon sells.

(Distance travelled: 40 miles. Profit: £400. Fact learned: Fortune can follow a rummage.)

Closing Down Bangor Bookshop, January 2007

My retail experience in Britain is drawing to an ignominious end. The philosophy had been the more books the merrier. Nine months ago a shipping container's doors had been flung apart to reveal 8 foot by 8 foot by 40 foot of emptiness. Drunk on the space and its book hoarding potential, I'd put down the deposit to rent it. I'd filled it with thousands of books and in the course of the last three months, I've emptied it of thousands of books. I open shops and later close them. Like Sisyphus, condemned by the gods to ceaselessly roll a rock to the top of a mountain (whence the stone would fall back of its own weight), I am forever buying and selling. I buy with ease but sell with difficulty, which is why the floor of the shop is now strewn with paper and print. I've given up any attempt at classification. People don't seem to mind the chaos. Over the years I've amassed all types of books including those that have little chance of selling. They are getting a last opportunity to find new homes and readers in my closing down sale.

I've also brought into the shop the Headington Circulating Library, with its biographies of knighted naval captains and Sabatini's and other books popular in the 1930s. Reflecting on the curious charm of the ragged remainders of the 'Headington Circulating Library', a customer called Ken, a modern day Socrates, is reminded of a passage in one of Lamb's 'Elia' essays. Charles Lamb, he tells me, was much given to bringing home 'tattered tomes' from the stalls in St Paul's churchyard two hundred years ago.

> 'How beautiful to a genuine lover of reading are the sullied leaves and worn-out appearances, nay the very odour (beyond Russia) if we would not forget kind feelings in fastidiousness, of an old Circulating Library 'Tom Jones,' or 'Vicar of Wakefield.' How they speak of the thousand thumbs, that have turned over their pages with delight!—of the lone sempstress, whom they may have cheered (milliner, or harder-working mantua-maker) after her long day's needle-toil, running far into midnight, when

she has snatched an hour, ill spared from sleep, to steep her cares, as in some Lethean cup, in spelling out their enchanting contents! Who would have them a whit less soiled? What better condition could we desire to see them in?'

An indefatigable reader and collector of books, Ken has a house that has long been considered a hospital for old or unfashionable books. It is having a wing added; a hospice for terminally damaged titles.

Bangor, 2008

An English priest with a scholarly obsession with Dickens is inspecting the twelve volume Pilgrim Edition of the author's letters. Delighted by their condition, the cash is soon splashed and I am informed that: 'The undertakers still only use cash you know.'

I feel relief that no offence is taken by a copy of *The God Delusion* nestling on the bookshelf. I don't want atheism to scupper the deal.

Djemea el Fna, Main Square in Marrakesh, 1993

In Marrakesh a man is shouted at for having the temerity to embrace his girlfriend at midday. He walks off, shrugging shoulders. Ramadhan means that there are no troupes of acrobats. There is, however, no shortage of other performers; a whole carnival of musicians, clowns and street entertainers. In fleeing a carefree snake charmer, I find myself accosted by Ramad who, after requesting and being denied money, is pleased just to chat. Over a coffee he tells me that his father is a maker of djellaba coats. Times are bad. 'La Misere partout. It was particularly bad during the Gulf war. The poor,' he says in hushed tones, 'are completed emasculated and people are wary of openly discussing politics. You end up in a big bag and are never seen again,' he says. There is a sudden blast of music. 'Rai from Algeria,' Ramad explains, gesturing to a nearby hall. We enter, and inside youngsters are dancing as if their lives depended on it. There is a real edge to the atmosphere that is absent from London nightclubs. It might come with knowing true desperation.

Leatherhead Hospice, 9 June 2005

'The most important thing I learned on Tralfamadore was that when a person dies he only appears to die. He is still very much alive in the past, so it is very silly for people to cry at his funeral. All moments, past, present and future, always have existed, always will exist. The Tralfamadorians can look at all the different moments just that way we can look at a stretch of the Rocky Mountains, for instance. They can see how permanent all the moments are, and they can look at any moment that interests them. It is just an illusion we have here on Earth that one moment follows another one, like beads on a string, and that once a moment is gone it is gone forever.

When a Tralfamadorian sees a corpse, all he
thinks is that the dead person is in bad condition
in the particular moment, but that the same
person is just fine in plenty of other moments.
Now, when I myself hear that somebody is dead, I
simply shrug and say what the Tralfamadorians
say about dead people, which is "so it goes".'

From *Slaughterhouse-Five* by Kurt Vonnegut Jr

Dad is a happy with his new room, especially its large window
through which he can see out onto the lawn outside. It makes
for a pleasant contrast to the environs of Kingston Hospital
from where he has been brought by ambulance today.

Diagnosed with motor neurone disease in February
(following a misdiagnosis of a stroke the previous month), he
has rapidly deteriorated; the pace of the disease catching
doctors, friends and family by surprise. His mind is unaffected
though and he wants to engage in conversation in spite of an
increasing inability to make intelligible sounds. We 'talk'
intermittently for hours on end until his breathing becomes
particularly laboured. After re-applying his oxygen mask, I go
off for a tour of the town.

Within ten minutes, I am ensconced in Dandy Lion Editions
Bookshop. Scanning the books for likely titles, I briefly forget the
reason for me being in Leatherhead. 'Action gives us consolation
for our inexistence,' opines John Gray in *Straw Dogs*.

I turn up a first edition copy of *The Selfish Gene*, a hugely
influential book on evolution by Richard Dawkins published in
1976. Dawkins coined the term 'selfish gene' as a way of
expressing the gene-centred view of evolution, which holds that
evolution is best viewed as acting on genes and that selection

at the level of organisms or populations almost never overrides selection based on genes.

I return to the hospice to show Dad my find. Always having praised Dawkins, he is pleased by both the book's subject matter and its potential financial return.

Dad has taken a keen and abiding interest in my efforts to make a living out of books. After his retirement, we sometimes worked in tandem during my bulk buying trips. Dashing across West London it felt like we were bank robbers; he waiting in the 'get away' car while I charged in and out of venues of potential pickings, dodging between the clothes hangers in charity shops.

He didn't object to his once plush flat resembling a grocer's stockroom; fruit and veg boxes, filled to the brim with books, piled up high in every corner.

A nurse enters the room to bring us tea. I hold the cup to his lips. 'Lovely,' I hear him rasp. We talk some more before I leave. He gives me, with difficulty, a thumbs up, and I tell him that I'll see him tomorrow. I do, but not as we both imagine. At dawn I receive a phone call from the hospice; a nurse gently informs me that he died in his sleep in the early hours.

I learn later that the Motor Neurone Disease Association uses a Thumbs Up symbol as its logo, representing David Niven's last defiant gesture.

La Comédie du Livres, Montpellier, May 1994

Dad has raced down with his car full of books. He excitedly relates his journey along the motorway across the Massif

Central, much of it running at an altitude in excess of 2600 feet, with 30 miles in excess of 3250 feet. Concentrating on my stand and rearranging the display of books upon it, I can't properly follow what he's saying. My focus is on replenishing the stand with *Calvin and Hobbes* (the comic strip, that is, not the philosophers) and English language *Tintins*.

This is the first year that I've participated in La Comédie du Livres, the largest book fair in southern France. I don't want to blow it. Tents and marquees cover the vast Place de la Comédie. Hundreds of writers, comic strip artists (big in France) and publishers, along with the local bookshops, have assembled to attract an enthusiastic public. The crowds swarm around the tents, seemingly immune to the day's stifling heat. We have protection from the sun's fierce rays; the awnings draped generously over the tent's metal framework.

Business is brisk for everybody. People are delighted to meet favourite writers and the atmosphere is conducive to book selling. Along with the books hauled in a panic late last night from my shop, the books from London mean that my stand boasts an impressive variety of titles. I'm selling to tourists and locals alike.

As booksellers, we have only to pay a nominal fee in order to participate in the fair, which is mostly subsidised by the council. The French certainly plough money into culture and they are protective of their book industry, having retained even the net book agreement. Dad is amazed to hear of the council's generosity and a journalist encourages him to air such views. Next week, a paragraph of his praise is printed in the local paper alongside his picture. '*Sur son stand de la Comédie du livre, le patron de "Bills Book Company" ressemble a un major… anglais of course! Plein d'humour, sourant, quand on lui* demande "ca march?" Il repond immanquablement, "very positive," et ajoute 'jamais en Angleterre on imaginerait qu'on subventionne les gens pour ce type d'operation".'

Other English people we meet at the event are similarly impressed, including athlete Roger Black, who has been training in the vicinity.

Towards the end of the day, I meet an American lady called Sophie Herr who has a weakness for Ellis Peters' novels. She becomes a regular at the shop. I learn that she has famous parents. Her mother, Caroline, was chiefly responsible for bringing the dancer Josephine Baker to Paris. She then met and married Joseph Delteil, a local author and poet held in high esteem. He thus became Sophie's stepfather. Sophie, it turns out, is a friend of George Whitman.

Disillusionment, Kingston Nightclub, 1986

Eddy wants to us to start in The Fox even though we usually drink here only on quiet nights. We find no offence in the slapdash paintings of boats stranded on mud-flats, the gaudily framed portrait of Winston Churchill at his most stoical. We drink, to build up Dutch courage, with dogged determination. A couple of women huddle around a cigarette machine. I feel a sudden attraction to one of them. I follow the play of light as her dark hair, cut in a page-boy style, swings out of synch. Her friend also seems mesmerised.

'Lovely girls. Shame they're not gonna be going to Pars,' says Eddy. 'They won't let anyone in with jeans.'

Night has quietly fallen outside The Fox. We are oblivious to the drop in temperature but we notice the altered appearance of the streets under artificial light. The street lamps glow yellow like deformed daffodils on metal stalks. We walk swiftly on.

The old Palais dance hall has undergone extensive structural alteration; an extra floor has been put in and two ends of the hall partitioned off in wedges to lend the room the shape of a parallelogram. There are four stroboscopes suspended from the ceiling. They shed a dazzling mix of light upon the dancing women.

'Ask her for a dance.'

'Don't be stupid. It's way too early.'

Eddy and I hover near the dance floor onto which few men have walked.

Somebody is pulling at my arm. Eddy is shouting, and through the drunken haze, I can just make it out the words: 'Is this it?'

La Comédie du Livres, Montpellier, May 1997

James Crumley's books have inspired a generation of crime writers. Over the Tannoy, his French publisher announces his presence on a stand near to mine. Dad agrees to hold the fort so that I can go and meet him. I've loved reading his fiction, which is a cross between Raymond Chandler and Hunter S. Thompson. Crumley has something of a cult following of which I'm a fully paid up member.

Rapt in conversation with an elderly man is Crumley's agent. Sitting in front of them is the man himself. Near to the table's edge is a bottle of pastis. And near to the pastis is a pile of books that await signing. My eyes meet his and I'm struck by how bloodshot they are. I strike up conversation after purchasing *Un pour marquer la cadence*, a French translation of his first published novel, 1969's *One to Count Cadence*, which is set in Vietnam. We chat. I explain what I'm doing here and attempt to convey my admiration for his writing without, I hope, slipping into sycophancy. He inscribes my copy. 'Bill – See you soon (for a beer) Jim Crumley Mai 1997'. I intend to do just that. But by the time I have packed away my books, he has been whisked away by his publisher.

Crumley's books feature either the character C. W. Sughrue, an alcoholic ex-army officer turned private investigator, or another PI, Milo Milodragovitch. In the novel *Bordersnakes*, Crumley brought both characters together. Of his two protagonists, Crumley says that 'Milo's first impulse is to help you; Sughrue's is to shoot you in the foot.' In our brief meeting, I detect in Crumley's character distinctly more of the Milo than the Sughrue.

Richmond, Surrey, 1989

Late on Wednesday, the natural light of the day is fading fast. Plumes of cigarette smoke spiral up from the desks. Phones ring intermittently. There are hurried conversations and a frantic finger dance on keyboards. My index fingers, too, contribute to this deadline rush of stories. The screen is lined with sentences I've just written. I stare at the green background enveloping the words. Imagining the greenness as an ocean, I wish crassly that the sentences be drowned in it. Jennifer has left. I can't really take it in. Are these precursor thoughts to a breakdown? Can I get insurance, 'nervous' breakdown cover? Crack up and be paid to convalesce somewhere nice? I stare, as if hypnotised by the freshly typed words that await punctuation. Must get going though. I type with demonic vigour, spewing out stories. I correct spelling mistakes before rearranging words, bringing them into accordance with the paper's style sheet. When using a typewriter, I did this job inside my head. But now I tend to write the first draft of a story in one big splurge of disordered thought.

I don't join the others for a drink after work. This upsets Eddy, who wants my company to divulge a confidence. It must wait. I want to visit my parents to break the news. I also like the idea of a good lounge in front of the television, mug of tea in hand.

There is no need to hurry but an inexplicable force impels me to ride the bike at top speed. A car swerves out into the middle of the road to avoid contact. I then realise that I have fallen into the spirit of competition, racing against cars and fellow cyclists. My heart pumps harder. I feel my back moisten with sweat. Pushing down aggressively on the pedals, I soon arrive. I park my bike in the alleyway that runs alongside the house. It is dank and full of derelict bikes, some of which have 'stabilisers' dating back to my infancy. There are bigger bikes stripped of various essential components like seats and cross bars. They make me think of skeletons awaiting burial. Mum resists organising their removal; it would signal the emphatic end of something quintessentially familial.

For some reason I forsake the lounge and tea. Instead I go out to stand in the cold garden. The shiftless clouds have come to harden my sense of frustration. I want sunshine. A beaker full of it and more. And I know what I don't want: fêtes, marriages, council meetings and supermarket openings. I can rid myself of it all by a single press of the 'Delete' button. I have come to tell them this.

Phil has given me a copy of Sartre's *Nausea*. A mistake, maybe, given my current solipsistic musings.

Tregarth Council Flat, North Wales, February 2003

We get the call. Along with a fellow bookseller, I have the chance to go through the library of a man who must leave his council house for a nursing home. We arrive to find the books in various corners of the house. Dan is happy to buy a handful but for me only one title stands out. *The Britannia and Conway Tubular Bridges* by Edwin Clark in two volumes. With *General Inquiries on Beams and on the Properties of Materials used in Construction.*

Some research is needed. Edwin Clark, it transpires, was the clerk of the project which built a bridge across the Menai Strait between the island of Anglesey and the mainland of Wales. The volumes contain descriptions and drawings of the original tubular bridge; with wrought iron rectangular box-section spans. It is now a two-tier steel truss arch bridge.

Clark produced a comprehensive presentation of continuous beam theory as applied to the Britannia and Conway bridges, backed up by experiments, within the scope of a two-volume book about both bridges, I am reliably informed. The work was published by Day & Son and John Weale, 1850. And with the sanction, and under the supervision, of Robert Stephenson.

Two vols. of text in 8vo, orig. blind-stamped cloth spines gilt. contents very good, spines worn and scuffed at top and bottom,

no markings, binding good; both volumes are heavy and we will
need to incorporate postage costs into the book price.

I take the book to a Llandudno dealer at the trade's top end. 'Museum stock', I say to Dan by way of explaining the man's credentials. The dealer expresses interest although there is some confusion as to whether there should be another volume. There is no mention, in the book we have, of a third volume, but COPAC – an online library catalogue giving access to major university, specialist and national libraries in the UK – suggests that there is a third volume.

In spite of a lingering doubt over a third volume's existence, the dealer agrees to part with hundreds of pounds.

The mystery ends appropriately enough within sight of Britannia Bridge several years later while taking a tour of Plas Newydd, a National Trust country house in Llanfairpwll, Anglesey. We have brought the kids to see Rex Whistler's drawings and the military museum with relics from the Battle of Waterloo. Here, in front of the former marquis's artificial leg, a Trust volunteer is railing on about the iniquities of Napoleon and his people. We allow him to finish his speech before revealing Anne's and our children's French nationality. Afterwards we pass into an anteroom where I spot, lying on an elegant mahogany table, a large leather bound volume with the words Britannia Bridge and Plates embossed upon its side. The book is of a larger format than the two volumes we have sold. The usher in the room breaks protocol; kindly permitting close examination. It is indeed the missing volume; an atlas complete with 47 lithographed plates (six tinted, five double-page and folding).

Plas Newydd, November 1993

Before opening a bookshop at Plas Newydd, the Trust used to organise an annual book sale event there in mid-November. Surrounding the house are large gardens, woodland walks and a marine walk along the Menai Strait where we bump into the current Marquis of Anglesey. He seems to be doing a spot of impromptu gardening, from which he breaks off to politely acknowledge us. 'It's a good book sale,' we say in passing. 'Good. Good. Buy lots of books,' he instructs in jovial fashion. We already have. Several hundred in fact. Dad has helped by being on hand to carry the books I pick out. You don't have much time when other dealers are engaged in the same activity. There are thousands of books; scanning their spines is exhilarating. The sheer pot luck of the experience; what author and what title will crop up? Pick and pass and scan. Pick and pass and scan. Your mind is racing. Recognising titles and estimating their resale value. Pick and pass and scan.

The Interaction of Books, Life and Death, Llanfihangel, Late August 2006

To the north and west of Llanfihangel are the high moorlands of the Berwyn, while south-eastwards the land falls towards the Vyrnwy and Severn valleys. Nain (my grandmother) was brought up in the area on a farm.

Her mother gave her a book entitled *Life in a Welsh Countryside – A Social Study of Llanfihangel yng Ngwynfa* by Alwyn D Rees. On page 86 is the following paragraph.

'Since the household is asleep when the young man appears on the premises, it is necessary to signal the girl, and this is done by throwing turf, gravel or dried peas at her window. Hence, the practice is called mynd I gnocio (going to knock). An appointment is not essential, a young man may go to knock up a girl to whom he has never spoken before. If he is lucky, she will come to the window, the young man will introduce himself, and if he is acceptable she will let him into the kitchen, and they will have a light meal or a cup of tea together. In Merioneth, the custom is called myn I gynnig (going to offer, or to try one's luck).

Priceless. I can't sell this book. Can I?

My Nain's ashes lie in the village cemetery. Today we are interring my father's ashes alongside. Family has assembled. My children recite a poem by R. S. Thomas.

The Bright Field
I have seen the sun break through
to illuminate a small field
for a while, and gone my way
and forgotten it. But that was the pearl
of great price, the one field that had
treasure in it. I realise now
that I must give all that I have
to possess it. Life is not hurrying
on to a receding future, nor hankering after

an imagined past. It is the turning
aside like Moses to the miracle
of the lit bush, to a brightness
that seemed as transitory as your youth
once, but is the eternity that awaits you.

I have some irreverent thoughts that I keep to myself. Earlier, in reading to myself the R. S. Thomas poem 'Gifts', I come across the line, 'From my father my strong heart' and I can't help but hear the word 'fart'. For diplomacy's sake, we do not use this poem. And we refrain from using another of Thomas's poems, 'Welcome to Wales', although this has lines that seem uncomfortably relevant. *Come to Wales / To be buried; the undertaker / Will arrange it for you. / We have the sites and a long line / Of clients going back.*

Years later, a dealer whose quarry was manuscripts and authors' letters contacts me. Believing me to have the 'right' name and connections, I am handed the following in February 2009.

Thomas (Ronald Stuart)
A small archive of mostly typed material, mostly early 1980s, including a rare cassette and material relating to a BBC Radio 3 broadcast in 1983 celebrating the 70th birthday of RS Thomas, including a rough sketch of the programme/script in the hand of Kevin Crossley-Holland. Twelve folio sheets, a further set of twelve leaves being a second sketch plan for the programme, heavily corrected by Crossley-Holland, plus a further forty-six pages

in his hand, a further revised version, typed interviews with D.Z. Phillips, Gwyn Jones, Robin Young, Andrew Waterman and R.S. Thomas himself, all with corrections by Crossley-Holland. Plus an original typescript of Thomas's book *Cymru or Wales?*, a related letter from the editor Meic Stephens, a short note in the poet's holograph written at the end of the letter with his signature, plus a thirteen page typescript of a broadcast by Thomas entitled 'The Living Poet.', from 17th November 1980.

Before submitting the R. S. Thomas material to auction, I decide to give Bangor University the opportunity to acquire the papers. The university has set up a special Research Centre which seeks 'to promote research into his work, the Centre's archive contains all of R. S. Thomas's published works, together with a comprehensive collection of reviews, critical books and articles, interviews and audio-visual material.'

There is some initial enthusiasm before their interest wanes. Maybe they have a surfeit of material.

Near to Llanfihangel is Llanfylin, which lies on the River Cain amid gently rolling hills. My Nain went to school in the village as did my father in the war years of the 1940s. We have spent happy days on holiday visiting family in the town.

Situated at the top of Greenhall hill, south east Llanfylin, is 'The Lonely Tree.' It stands above Y Dolydd workhouse and legend has it that if you intend to stay in the area, you must make the trek up the hill to give the tree a hug. Whenever I read 'Fern Hill', I think of great afternoon expeditions, as they seem to us then as children, to reach 'The Lonely Tree'. Used to London streets, we saw the countryside as so exotic, with its gigantic ferns in which we could hide.

> *Fern Hill*
> Now as I was young and easy under the apple boughs
> About the lilting house and happy as the grass was green,
> The night above the dingle starry,
> Time let me hail and climb
> Golden in the heydays of his eyes,
> And honoured among wagons I was prince of the apple towns
> And once below a time I lordly had the trees and leaves
> Trail with daisies and barley
> Down the rivers of the windfall light.

My cure for feeling blue in Paris is to visit the Pompidou Centre and listen to recordings of the poem made by the author. I recall an oceanography field trip to Laugharne lying on the estuary of the River Tâf. The town is widely known for having been the home of Dylan Thomas and may have been an inspiration for the fictional town of Llareggub in *Under Milk Wood*.

As oceanography students, we dyed the beaches by day (to detect movements in the sands) and drank beer by night in what was Dylan's 'local' – Brown's Hotel. We were let out of a lock in, which means that our 3 a.m. walk down to the beach was really a drunken stagger. A couple of no good boyos up to no good. Joe wanted to 'contribute' to the experiment by peeing on the sand in the test area.

English Bookshops and a Mexican Restaurant, Paris, 1990

I'm suffering from the would-be writer's delusion of waiting for the muse to visit; hoping that the ghosts of Hemingway and Joyce will work their magic. I'm in Paris to check out the English book scene and am wondering if can get a job connected to it. I visit the city's legendary Shakespeare and Company, an independent bookshop located in the fifth arrondissement, in Paris's Left Bank. Its octogenarian owner George Whitman keeps the shop open late into the night and you can find work but only in exchange for accommodation. George thinks of his temporary tenants – 'tumbleweeds' – as budding writers; they are required to read a book a day as part of the deal which allows them to sleep in the shop among the shelves of books.

The original proprietor was Sylvia Beach and her shop was located at 12 rue de l'Odéon. The shop was frequented by artists of the 'Lost Generation', such as Ernest Hemingway, Ezra Pound, Scott Fitzgerald, Gertrude Stein and James Joyce. Shakespeare and Company, as well as its literary denizens, was repeatedly mentioned in Hemingway's *A Moveable Feast*, a paperback which I automatically buy whenever I come across a copy out of a strange sense of loyalty to my memories of Paris, as well as those of Hemingway's. Not that I remotely equate the two.

It was Sylvia Beach who first published Joyce's book *Ulysses* in 1922. The book was subsequently banned in the United States and United Kingdom. The original Shakespeare and Company published several other editions of *Ulysses* under its imprint in later years. D. H. Lawrence wanted Sylvia Beach to published *Lady Chatterley's Lover*, to hamper the circulation of an unauthorised edition doing the rounds in Paris. She refused Lawrence's *Lady*, citing a lack of capital and time. She later wrote that it was 'impossible to say that I wanted to be a one-book publisher, what could anybody offer after *Ulysses*?'

One morning eight years later, in March 2000, a lady strides through the doors of my shop in Montpellier to drop off a plastic bag bulging with books. '*Cadeaux*' she shouts, before walking swiftly back out. Such donations aren't that uncommon. In having a good clear out, people regularly come by to 'dump' their unwanted English books. I encourage the practice, as there are usually some books worth saving. This time the bag is stuffed with old textbooks of limited usefulness, but below them, nestling at the bottom of the bag, is a large, and unusual paperback.

Ulysses: Shakespeare and Company, 1924. Original cover (white with blue lettering). 4 page corrections bound in at rear of volume. 8th Printing. Original Blue wrappers.

It didn't stay long in the shop, a dealer in Joyce taking it off my hands. I was going to write that the book returned to Ireland. But it didn't, of course, as a physical object, hail from Dublin, although its characters did. Joyce's thoughts were rarely in exile.

The sale's proceeds of £400 were shared with my then business partner.

Back to Paris, and a gruff sounding George is explaining Tumbleweed Hotel's modus operandi. He invites me to lunch but I make my excuses and leave. Oddly enough, I don't feel that comfortable in the bookish atmosphere and being around so many bohemian types. I also realise that there is no paid work on offer.

I get a friendly reception in Tea and Tattered Pages, a retail concept I later adopt in Montpellier. But they say, almost apologetically, that there are no jobs going.

Abbey Bookshop, a small shop specialising in Canadian books and literature, certainly doesn't raise any expectations either.

Nearby is another shop in the vicinity of the Sorbonne which I come across by accident. I recognise its name – Attica – and inside the shop its manager explains that it is the sister business, as it were, of the shop in Rue Folie Méricourt in the eleventh arrondissement, an establishment selling foreign language textbooks in the main and teaching aids.

David is decidedly foppish with his smart linen jacket and blond hair which he is forever sweeping back from his forehead. He is in his early thirties and articulate in English while retaining a strong French accent. Holding forth is a long-haired, dark complexioned American student called Jan. He talks intensely about the utilitarianism of the Red Indians and David is listening with a distracted air to stories of buffalo being forced off cliffs. (I think the conversation owes its origin to the imminent release of Kevin Costner's *Dances with Wolves*.) In ascertaining that Jan is soon to return home, I sense there may be a job opportunity. I buy some books, including *Money* by Martin Amis, which is probably a subconscious choice, and end up staying a while since David is in chatty mood. He's pleased to hear that I'm from London. He's quite the anglophile and I soon learn that he used to live with an

'East End girl'. I exaggerate my city boy credentials and get offered a couple of afternoons' work a week.

David likes to play the generous host; his benevolence extending to books. *The Road to Oxiana* by Robert Byron is one of his early gifts. It brilliantly recounts the author's journey through the Middle East to Oxiana – the country of the Oxus, the ancient name for the river Amu Darya, which forms part of the border between Afghanistan and the Soviet Union. It stirs the wanderlust. We travel to Chartres; our travelling ambitions not extending to buying a plane ticket to Kabul. We marvel at the Gothic architecture which years later will be a comforting sight on my travels between France and the UK. The immense cathedral is visible from miles away as you approach it by road through the surrounding flat fields of wheat. Within five minutes of the town's historical heart is the camp-site Les bords de l'Eure, situated beside the gently flowing waters of the Eure – where I will regularly stay in years to come since it conveniently breaks up the journey between Montpellier and Bangor.

Ostensibly, I make sure that the books are arranged in alphabetical order. My real task, I suspect, is to alleviate David's boredom. The shop isn't that busy and the only regulars are a motley crew of characters, myself included, who rarely leave with purchased books. There is a tall Irish aristocrat who could be a character straight out of a J. P. Donleavy novel. Outspoken and on the wrong side of thirty, he is considerable older than his livewire Serbian girlfriend, whose outrageous ideas mix madness and brilliance. They are scathing in their opinion of George Whitman after spending eight years as 'tumbleweeds' before falling out with him. Whitman's current head honcho is Karl. Ernest and intellectual, he is a much calmer presence. When he isn't working at Shakespeare and Company, he is publishing books through his own press called Alyscamps. Serendipity runs through our lives and the book world is no exception. Karl publishes in 1994 *A Dream in the Luxembourg* by Richard Aldington with a preface by Lawrence Durrell. The following year Richard Adlington's daughter walks into my shop. I know that many consider the central idea in John Guare's *Six Degrees of Separation* to be an urban myth. But my experiences suggest that its premise is plausible. That if a person is one step away from each person they know and two steps away from each person who is known by one of the people they know, then everyone is at most six steps away from any other person on Earth.

Some sort of deal has been struck. George Whitman turns up at Attica with a couple of 'tumbleweeds' in tow (both American girl students) who each carry a large 'mail' sack. David exits the shop for a cigarette and George is soon shuffling around, nonchalantly pulling books, mostly paperbacks, from the shelves. He lets them fall to the floor and the girls obligingly bend down to pick them up. It is an astonishing sight. This bearded and elderly gentleman muttering to himself as he peruses the shelves, setting off mini avalanches of paper up and down the shop. He continues in this fashion until the girls protest at the weight of the bags.

David hovers by the till and this appears to be the signal for George to produce a thick wad of notes. It isn't to buy my silence that, following the 'Whitman raid', David hands me a couple of 100 franc notes. It's more his embarrassment, I think, at me having witnessed a transaction involving so much dosh in relation to my meagre wage. He knows that I can't live on the hours that he gives me in the shop.

I have to do an Orwell.

Relevant experience, claimed to secure the job at La Tavern Mexicaine, is quickly exposed as the lie that it is. The manager, Jean-Pierre, however, is perversely pleased; ineptitude rendering me good haranguing material. I can be relied upon to 'fuck up'. His unnerving presence means that there is the constant threat of a bellowed instruction. 'Six guacamole, six nachos. *Non, non; non. J'ai dit deux, oui deux taco poulet. T'es con?*' The question is in all likelihood directed towards me since Raja has been sent to collect meat packages from a giant refrigerator in the backyard. Apart from me, the kitchen work force is Sri Lankan, men who have fled from the turmoil afflicting their country. 'We had to,' is all Raja says on the matter, making it clear that he has no intention of revealing more about the nature of their exile.

In spite of his competence, Raja is especially targeted since he is able to convey a sense of irony at his slavishness. I observe the battle between the boss and the bossed. Raja smokes illicitly in the backyard, mounts food raids on the stores and furtively mocks the manager by pulling faces. But Jean-Pierre, as if in retaliation, set tasks that are designed to humiliate. Raja is required to re-stack neatly stacked buckets, wash clean plates, and he is admonished for dicing vegetables the wrong size. '*T'es con?* The onions, I can't see them.'

Both are French – the manager and the chef, a man who excels not in tyranny but in propagating a mood of sullenness. So it is in the spirit of subtle rebellion that I find myself speaking to the Sri Lankans about cricket. When fed up or stressed, I find sport often to be an effective palliative. In *A Fan's Notes*, its author Frederick Exley asks 'Why did football bring me so to life? I can't say precisely. Part of it was my feeling that football was an island of directness in a world of circumspection.' (Incidentally, *A Fan's Notes* always sells well despite there being quite a few copies knocking about in the Penguin edition.) He was talking about American football but the quote holds true for other sports. That's why I am excited about our mutual interest in cricket. The Sri Lanka cricket team is touring England. The newspaper, which I buy on the morning that the first test is scheduled to start, charitably defines their threat to England as one more subtle than that posed by the West Indians. My work colleagues excitedly run through their team's line up before their thoughts turn briefly to the opposition. The mention of Gooch and Gower causes them to nod with respectful solemnity.

Our cricket conversations (invariably mine were with Raja) strike me as incongruous amid the cacophony of kitchen sounds: knives striking marble chopping boards, the clanging clash of tray on floor and the near constant hum of an industrial dishwasher. Electing to bat first, Sri Lanka play with a carefree abandon that rules out a big innings. My colleagues are not really disappointed when England win and cricket continues to provides a focus for communication between us. Raja is awesomely accurate as a bowler, sending down unplayable deliveries between the stoves. He insists that Ragunathan, positioned in front of the dishwasher, has caught me out at third slip.

At the start of the week, Raja is in fine form, both with the imaginary ball and with life in general. He has got one over Jean-Pierre by finding employment for a cousin who has recently arrived in Paris. Raja has circumvented the manager's authority by making his request direct to restaurant's Head of Personnel, a woman with an easy-going disposition that I find difficult to reconcile with the atmosphere of the kitchen. After a shift, she doesn't mind if we stuff ourselves, almost to the point of sickness, with steaks and tostadas. Three of the Sri Lankans have been chef assistants for two years, their lithe bodies testament to the calories burnt up in the course of a hard working day. I mutilate the vegetables whereas they stroke them into slices. They have acquired an unassuming strength that rips lids noiselessly off buckets containing ingredients. I am adapting to the work but remain cack-handed in comparison to them. Going about their kitchen business with impressive efficiency, they do their best to make me feel part of the kitchen brotherhood. I am tipped off if the manager is on the warpath. I am invited to partake in covert food snacks.

On that final morning, Raja and myself are up to our necks in tomatoes. Since the place is going to be understaffed in the evening, two additional crates of big juicy tomatoes await dissection. I am first to complain. This makes Raja explain, by way of offering consolation, that the task is an even worse one in January. The glossy skinned tomatoes are tougher then and finger numbing cold. 'But it's not algebra.' Nothing is ever as difficult as algebra.

Raja's temperament is undergoing a transformation. The manager has spent his morning spitting his foulness with evil efficacy. '*Propreté and rapiditié*,' he has bellowed. '*T'es con*?' It is as if Raja's high spirits earlier in the week have exacerbated the vindictive side to the manager's nature. And the verbal attack is sustained further, during the heat and panic of a major lunch time rush. Raja says nothing, but beads of sweat break out upon his forehead.

Finally it happens. I am on my knees, looking for a 10-franc coin that has dropped out of my chequered chef trousers. The manager is inspecting plates before waiters whisk them away.

According to Jean-Pierre's arbitrary system of measurement, Raja is dumping excessively copious portions of *degustacion de pacifico* on the plates. 'You try to make us poor,' he complains. 'Call this plate clean, you useless fuck?' The language doesn't surprise me as I get to my feet, expecting another broadside, but Jean-Pierre is otherwise preoccupied. Raja has him pinned against a shelf. The steel blade of the knife is of proven sharpness, reddened with vestigial tomato skin and juice. A thrilling uncertainty reigns for a moment, the manager grimacing with fright. But in sensing that if Raja is going to strike, he would already have done so, he recovers his composure. With a sad air of contrition, Raja withdraws the knife from the fleshy throat. The manager, along with the rest of us, watches silently as Raja walks out of the kitchen and then out of the restaurant. The next day I, too, walk out after shouting abuse in his face *'T'es con con con con.'* My voice is breaking up. I tremble with the nervous energy. I've spent 24 hours working myself up to this moment. I am expecting a big scene. But Jean-Pierre, completely unfazed, says it is good for me to go. 'You better off teaching.' When I return a week later for my pay cheque, Ragunathan tells me that Raja has found a job in an Indian restaurant but that the steam cooking is making him unwell.

Two days after the Raja knife incident I go to church: the American Church besides the Quai d'Orsay, or rather an annexe of it where English and Americans congregate in their quest to find accommodation and/or employment. 'Dishwasher wanted.' Of the human variety, I take it. Three hours a day plus meal. Dish washing – how difficult can it be? I pass the phone interview but can't start for two weeks, which is when the *'plongeur'* will leave the post at a Montparnasse creperie.

Rue du Cheval Vert, Montpeller, Mid 1990s

Buoyed and encouraged by some good Sunday puces (markets), I decide to open a bookshop in Montpellier. There is already an English bookshop but they do not sell second-hand books.

Anne and I scour the city for locations and plump for a road (rue du Cheval Vert) near to a cinema, which screens American and English language films. By chance, the building at No. 3 in the road is where Napoleon's father met his maker. It says so on the plaque outside.

'*Ici est mort le 24 Fevrier 1785 Charles Bonaparte père de Napoléon 1er.*' Customers, thinking it somehow fitting for *un britannique* to set up shop here, occasionally allude to the plaque. Some even think that it accounts for the shop's location.

We jump through all the hoops: applying for a Carte de Sejour, registering with Montpellier's Chamber of Commerce, signing up to '*les charges sociales*'. We discover, to our dismay, that the social security contributions expected from a small business are much higher in France than in the UK.

The landlords are baffled by my business plan but willing to sign a 3-6-9 lease, which means I am responsible for paying the shop's rent for three years, after which I can renew or choose to leave. It's quite a responsibility because the lease is in my name. I am trading not as a limited company (SARL), but as a sole trader because it is easier to set up and makes for less complicated accounting. So I am told.

And then it's all go. Decoration. Assembling of shelves. Thinking of a name.

A friend suggests 'Leaves of Grass', which has a provocative appeal. Bill's Book Company is another suggestion. I would like to be associated with the cultured brand of the BBC. I chicken out from using their logo but hope that people will make the connection with the initials. BBC – Bill's Book Company.

A sign is made and then fastened above the shop of modest proportions. To attract the attention of ex-pats we stick jars of Marmite and a Paddington Bear in the window. The Penguin rep is sceptical of my decision to mix some new books with second-hand but she is won over on her first visit. The opening day is also a success, family and friends helping to make it so. Some customers even become good friends, lending support. In addition to making a pavement sign, bass guitarist Beach applies his artistic talents to designing flyers. The novelty of English second-hand books sees me through the opening months. But then we enter the summer months, long hot ones. Compensating a little for the students' and locals' annual desertion, the tourist trade ensures survival. And I'm pleased to soon feature in some of the budget guidebooks to France.

> *Let's Go* 1995
> Bills Book Company (BBC) 9 rue du Cheval Vert (tel: 67 22 79 09), off pl. St. Denis. Diverse and exciting collection of literary bijoux. Some new, but mostly second-hand paperbacks (9–20F) Bill the British proprietor, is always up for tea and a chat. Open Mon-Fri 9.30am–12.30pm and 2.30–6.30 pm, Sat. 9.30am–6.30pm'

Not that I'm fighting the hoards away. In August few people visit the shop. I call this time of the year 'The Burial of Hope for the Bookseller'.

The inactivity leads to idle speculation on money spinning ventures. I have a recurring fantasy set in a village near Millau (where Derek Raymond laboured in between the writing his Factory series). We occupy the bar terraces in the shade of the square afforded by the plane trees. We marvel at the sunny weather and enthuse about the red wines. We eat, drink and love excessively and what with our novel amounts of leisure, a mood of hedonism prevails for the duration of the holiday. We pretend to compensate for this indulgence by undertaking modest walks in the soporific heat. And of course we get touristy kicks from accomplishing simple everyday tasks, the foreign language negating the banality one normally associates with the daily chores such as a trip to the bakers.

We meet the village's mayor and self-appointed local historian.

'Oh yes, it had been an important spot once. Talagout was the market town of the valley, with three hundred and thirty three houses to be exact, and a dream of a church. I remember crying the day, in 1955, they drowned it all,' he says breathlessly. The lake was later leased out to a water company but the land and the reservoir itself remained state owned. So they didn't just flog them off like ours back home.

A *notaire* had grouped together all the houses for the sale. And the French State had forced L'Arnack, being the nearest village, into making the purchase. Financial compensation was dispensed to the inhabitants of Talagout, a sum of money still hotly disputed. L'Arnack's mayor hadn't wanted to buy the village for fear of appearing to condone the scheme, but the Government had forced his hand.

'Whenever a property is put on sale in France, the town council always has first option to buy. It prevents ludicrously low bids,' he explains. We are amazed to hear of such municipal power.

'In Britain the mayor is traditionally one of the more ineffectual councillors who get worked up over bottle banks and parking meters. They carry little clout, their post being basically an honorary one.' Following an explanation of the word clout, the discussion develops with the mayor striving to impress upon his listeners the magnitude of his legal clout.

'In the strictest terms of the mayor's mandate, you could sell Talagout then,' we deduce with mischievous glee. At that moment a transaction becomes a possibility. 'The village fête is in two days time. Let's make its sale the central event,' exclaims the by now grandiloquent mayor.

It rests on a roll of the dice. The old mayor is giggling uncontrollably, aware that a five is going to be difficult to beat. The pastis, council subsidised for the village fête, has robbed him of any residual air of municipal dignity he might once have possessed. The aniseed liquor heightens further the crazy notion of the 'old village' being at stake. 'A three,' he excitedly declares amid the approving roars of the revellers. We both search our pockets for the one franc needed, egged on by a drunken crowd. The 'old village' is ours. The mayor, reckless with age and alcohol, retrieves the deeds. And with the official stamp of the *Mairie*, Talagout village is sold to us for '*le franc symbolique*'.

Two days later the mayor has sobered. He isn't sure of the exact legal position but he reasons it pretty academic. The sale might even generate publicity for the region, which owes its prosperity as much to tourism as it does to the grape. It might also help their recently hatched project to twin the town, I suggest. '*Entente cordiale* and all that.'

I get down to a new business. Estate Agency.

A GREAT EUROPEAN PROPERTY DEAL: 333 house village in
South of France for sale. Extensive renovation work required.
Derelict since 1955. Lovely surrounding vineyards in hilly
countryside. Exceptionally humid climate. Consult us.

By the last week of August, I am convinced that my fortune lies
in writing a spoof detective novel that breaks all the rules as
laid down by Father Knox. I discover, in a pamphlet on the
crime fiction genre written by Julian Symons, that in 1929 the
clergyman produced a list of the ten Commandments of
Detective Fiction. They are as follows:

1   The detective must be mentioned early on
2   Supernatural solutions are ruled out
3   Only one secret room or passage is allowed
4   No undiscovered poisons are permitted
5   No Chinamen should appear in the story
6   The detective must not be helped by lucky accidents, or by
    intuitions
7   The detective must not himself commit the crime
8   Nor must he conceal clues from the reader
9   The thoughts of 'The Watson' must not be concealed
10 There must be a special warning of the use of twin
    brothers or doubles

In my crime novel, an English protagonist will be undone by
cultural differences. For example, an Englishman would expect
to be able to leave his front door without needing a key. A
French front door could trap him.

In fact Josef Škvorecký, Czech writer and publisher, has
already harvested a book from the Commandments. His *Sins for*

Father Knox, published in 1991, comprises ten stories (two featuring Lieutenant Boruvka) in which a crime occurs that violates one of Father Knox's rules, thus serving up a double challenge: Who dunnit? and Which rule was broken? An Amazon reviewer says that the 'result is a genuinely innovative, brain-teaser of a novel that pokes fun at American pulp fiction.'

Having an idea, but not the application nor the actual talent to follow it through, is a prevailing theme in my life. There are so many distractions. Years later, in my second shop, the internet proves another distraction. I even find time to submit haikus to *The Guardian* online.

> want to win a prize?
> encapsulate news events
> in three simple lines

> a haiku headline
> snapshot of the world today
> elucidation

The site contains haiku of the day, featured poets, and a rejection of the 5-7-5 restrictions. The best topical haiku received will be posted on the site, and each week the overall winner will net its author £20 worth of Penguin Classics. Great. Free stock. But I never actually win, in spite of repeated attempts and a developing obsession. I even get a friend 'John' to have a go. Honourable mentions to...

> Off-colour health news
> White doctors better treated
> NHS disease.
>
> William Rees

Paddington Hatfield
There's blood on the Railtrack STOP
All Change to Corbett

William Rees

Now summer is here
Noisy kids sweltering nights
Solstice? Bag o'shite!

John Cleary

Euston Train Station, 4 October 2009

We are rushing to catch the 15.05 Chester train when I catch a glimpse of the Mayor of London. The stooped stance and shock of blond hair. It is undoubtedly Boris Johnson. He is looking a little lost. In taking our seats, we see him walking alone on the platform adjacent to our train. I surmise that he is awaiting the Manchester train in order to attend the Tory Party Conference and make mischief.

On the 6th of October, I send the following e-mail:

Dear Boris Johnson,

I intended to speak to you at Euston Station on Sunday afternoon but I was unable to do so. I was rushing, with my son, to get the Chester train. I wanted to tell you that I enjoyed your recent nomination and subsequent contribution to Radio 4's 'Great Lives'. It occurred to me that you might be interested in purchasing a painstaking facsimile of the first edition of Johnson's Dictionary that I have for sale. Price £600. Below is a description of the item.

The Folio Society, 2006. Hardcover. Book Condition: Fine. Johnson's Dictionary is an absolute triumph. Even the process used to tan the calf hides for the superb, three-quarter binding is the same as that which was used in Dr. Johnson's time. The boards and page edges are marbled by Ann Muir, reproducing a feature also found on the original. The colours used in my copy are shades of very dark green, red, several of ochre, and white. This palette perfectly complements the colours in the leather, the spine labels, and the paper. The same colour of paper is used, but it is of a much better quality, to ensure use by successive generations. The size is also faithful to the original and is, in a word, huge. The two, massive volumes weigh in at twenty-six pounds and require some effort to lift or carry about. All the hand work is of the highest degree of craftsmanship: the paper (Favini), the printing (St. Edmundsbury Press), the leather (Graham Wright Leather dappled calf), the binding (Smith Settle), the blocking and label work on the spine, the gloriously beautiful marbled covers and book edges (Ann Muir), and the scalloped case with its volume divider.

Should this e-mail spark any interest, please don't hesitate to contact me.

Yours faithfully

William Rees

On the 14th of October, I receive the following reply:

Dear Mr Rees,

The Mayor thanks you for your email. He has no plans to buy the volumes at the moment, but he has asked me to thank you for tipping him off.

Very best wishes,

Yours sincerely,
Ann Sindall
Executive Assistant to the Mayor

By strange coincidence, a London customer purchases the dictionary the very same day.

Collis School fête, Teddington, 2001

I head to the tables that have books piled upon them. Friendly volunteers man the stall.

I tend to smile benignly without entering into conversation. I can't allow myself to be distracted from what is essentially my work. 'You're a big reader,' I am told. I nod. Sometimes I come clean and declare my hand but not on this occasion. I put down a pile of James Bond paperbacks (Pan) so as to inspect a neat collection of early (but not Firsts) *Dr Dolittles*, each with a pristine dust wrapper. Nearby is a C. S. Lewis, *The Last Battle*, that looks like an early edition. It's seemingly in very good condition with its wrapper intact. My mind, upon turning the cover, prepares itself for disappointment, expecting to see any of the following: a torn page, a missing page, a library stamp, a reprint edition, a pen mark, an inscription, a previous owner's signature, spotting, a water stain, a price clipped d/j, a remainder mark, mould, bug damage.

None of them. Which is why I can describe it as a 'good collector's copy': cover slightly faded, no chips, no tears, book with illustrations in text, without inscriptions. Illustrator Pauline Baynes, published by The Bodley Head, 1956. *The Last Battle* concludes the Chronicles of Narnia. It deals with the end of time in the old Narnia and sums up the series by linking the experience of the human children in Narnia with their lives in their original world. This copy is on sale for £480.

It's started to drizzle so I carefully place the book inside my jacket. The weather isn't dampening anyone's zeal. People are tucking into fairy cakes. Jam is for sale. The bouncy castle is in operation and other children participate in the egg and spoon races. I think of my son back in France. His school too has fêtes, with tombolas and face painting. But there's something quintessentially English about egg and spoon and three-legged challenges. Mathieu attends l'Ecole Rudyard Kipling; the French naming many educational establishments after famous artists and writers.

I take him to the school gates where we loiter until a friend calls out. The shout from the other side of the playground exerts its pull. Matty pauses, for just a second or so, before charging off in zig zag fashion. He reminds me of a fish returned to the river, a moment to reacquaint itself with the water before that dart to freedom.

73

Scourie, Scotland, March 1990

A friend from university works on a salmon farm off the northwest coast of Scotland. His boss is prepared to buy a library of academic books on fisheries, and a more general selection concerning the physiology of fish. I neglect to mention that the books have come out of a skip, jettisoned by the college's accountants. It happens more frequently than you'd think.

I arrive late but there is just enough light to take in the barren hills bounding the loch. Sombre green waters are patched with wood and wire. Mark lives in a house within fifty yards of the loch. Ravaged by the elements, it is fast advancing towards dilapidation. Over a fish supper, Simon explains that I have an invitation from his boss to join in tomorrow's cull. There's a knock at the door. 'That'll be Jake,' says Mark. Jake lives with his sister in a white cottage nearby.

After a cold night it's good to be up and moving. There is time only for the briefest of introductions to Alex who says he'll check out the books after work. I have left them in the boot of the Princess, which has defied expectations in getting me here, a journey of some 700 miles from London.

We walk to the water's edge. Jake fights to light a cigarette. The lines of age curve chaotically all over his narrow reddened face. Swathed in dirty yellow oilskins, he crouches to get down low in the boat. By resting his good arm against the gunwale, Jake smokes, free of the wind's interference. He is shocked out of his reverie when the boat rocks with the sudden presence of Alex. Mark and I hurry to board the boat as its engine is jolted to life. I keep my eyes fixed to the metal gangway. Slip, and the sea will numb every nerve in the body.

Death is unlikely – providing you're fished out within five minutes.

His fingers glow red with defiance. Paralysed with arthritis and yellowed with nicotine, Jake's hand is little more than a cigarette holder. The good arm attains an equilibrium of sorts, but his body still shakes, needs more than a dram to control its mutinous movements.

'You all right lads?' he asks with vigour.

'Not too bad,' I lie. Jake had called round with a bottle of malt, which didn't see out the night.

'You'll not be inquiring after my welfare lads?' says Jake, who I now know has the capacity to drink a loch full of Glenfiddich.

'How are you feeling?' we say in chorus to which Jake replies 'Fucking awful. Spring time in Scotland. Hah!' he adds, looking around. Clouds scud across the sky, darkening the day. The sun can only shed a cold light upon the perennially soggy Highlands.

Salmon swim sluggishly. Jake sees too many salmon in his life; his clear blue eyes stare into the nets, rigidly secured and weighted down. In total there are twelve nets, aligned in two rows either side of an aluminium gangway wrapped in meshing. At one end, looking as if it had been tapped on as an afterthought, floats a shed where refuge is sought when storms stir.

In the boat we laboriously scoop and scatter foul smelling yellow pellets, using short handled shovels to extract them from big plastic bags. Adorning the bags is a picture of a salmon arched athletically above BP's insignia.

We saturate the salmon congested waters with mackerel, processed at great expense, Alex has told me, and then compressed into tablet form. Each bag contains seventy pounds of mackerel. Wrist muscles throb. We diligently scatter the pellets in an even spread, whereas Jake isn't above surreptitiously tipping out, in one cumulative plop, all the contents of the bag.

The waves are rising, but haven't yet reached a menacing height. The boat chugs contentedly enough towards a more sheltered part of the loch where the company holds the bigger salmon captive. Today there is to be a harvest. Lorries descend on the company's station, two inlets down the jagged coastline.

Some landlocked lakes teem with tiny salmon, tricked into accepting the freshwater environment as the river stage of their life cycle. Simon says that hired helicopters haul these fish out to be conveyed rapidly to salt loch waters. Chemicals in the tablets will turn the farm reared salmon the pink colour that wild salmon acquire naturally.

'How many?' asks Jake.

'A biggy. One thousand six hundred,' Alex answers, probably thinking of his bonus. Mark sighs, appreciating the magnitude of the toil involved. The wind strengthens. Tethered to the platform, the boat begins to pitch and roll. We watch the approach of a barge carrying crates half filled with ice. The barge is being pulled along by a squat craft powered by a noisy engine. The crew is a youthful bunch of burly locals. They assemble two waist-high benches near the crates before untying the ropes. One net is heaved upwards, so as not to disturb an outer net, which is interwoven with wire to deprive the seals of an easy meal.

The salmon splash madly, as if sensing their fate. Self-torpedoing, the salmon are easily ensnared in landing nets. The fish are tipped out, wriggling and gasping, onto the first bench, soon slippery with the slime of blood, scales and water. Clasped by their tails, the fish are dealt blows by Alex's club-wielding gang. Only the heads are battered, the odd eye is dislodged.

When they are flung onto the second bench, it is then our job to propel the dead and dying fish into the ice packed crates while keeping count. It is tiring work. Once begun, the cull always needs to be completed.

The barge is set loose on the sea, bound for the old barn that reeks of creosote. Beside the barn is a slipway, marking the culmination of a sharply undulating road that runs behind Jake's cottage. It tests the nerve of the lorry drivers charged with transporting the fish to supermarket.

We sit in the floor of the shed, which inside is lined with posters that show the various stages of sea lice infestation. Mark makes the tea while Jake and Alex eat Mars Bars. Farming the seas burns calories. Alex is pleased with the haul.

'How much do you want for the books?' His question takes me by surprise. I hope he'll appreciate the effort I'm putting in. I try my luck.

'Three hundred pounds?'

Okay. Deal done. Simon thinks Alex wants the books more for show, to give a sheen of intellect to a job that is essentially labour intensive.

I find it difficult to envisage Jake trudging back out for the afternoon feed.

But he does. The rain stings our faces as we go our separate ways, dragging bags to our assigned nets. On we work. Black smoke is coiling into the sky. The company is burning the discarded plastic bags.

A Book and a Memory,
Chirk Castle Bookshop, 2004

Madeleines, dipped in tea, are famous for sparking involuntary memories in Proust's novel *À la recherche du temps perdu* (*Remembrance of Things Past* in the first translation, more recently translated as *In Search of Lost Time*).

'She sent out for one of those short, plump little cakes called petites madeleines, which look as though they had been moulded in the fluted scallop of a pilgrim's shell. And soon, mechanically, weary after a dull day with the prospect of a depressing morrow, I raised to my lips a spoonful of the tea in which I had soaked a morsel of the cake. No sooner had the warm liquid, and the crumbs with it, touched my palate than a shudder ran through my whole body, and I stopped, intent upon the extraordinary changes that were taking place... at once the vicissitudes of life had become indifferent to me, its disasters innocuous, its brevity illusory...'
Remembrance of Things Past, Volume 1: Swann's Way.

Books possess that madeleine-like power. The second book that I truly read of my own volition (the first being *Shark Attack: Terrifying True Accounts of Shark Attacks*) was Muhammad Ali's 1975 autobiography, *The Greatest*. In it, Ali recounts his life, both in and out of the ring. The beauty of a great athlete whose family roots in Louisville fascinated me as much as his sporting endeavours. And Ali's victory over Foreman was, for me, an early experience of pure vicarious exhilaration. The book reminds me instantly of that night in 1974. Still decades after its publication, a mere glimpse of it – the yellow background and *The Greatest: My Own Story* in bold black type – transports me back to when Ali is taking a pummelling. Convinced that Ali's demise is imminent, my family and their friends have left the room. Round Eight. A punch is landed. They come rushing back into the room to sample the magic of the moment; the commotion in Zaïre able to emanate from a TV set in a Devon cottage. It's contagious; causing a ten-year old with no real interest in boxing to jump around and chant 'Ali! Ali! Ali!'

A Heinous Suggestion, Bangor, November 2009

Transhumance is the seasonal movement of people with their livestock, typically to higher pastures in summer and to lower valleys in winter.

It's getting cold at home in the attic rooms that have no central heating. We bring the computer down to the first floor, where the room temperature is more clement.

There is still a fireplace in the attic though. An acquaintance suggests we 'could always burn some books'.

Madrid, 1991

Murphy's *English Grammar in Use* is something of a bible for the community of teachers of English as a foreign language. As there seems to be large mark up on books sold in the shops here, I make inquiries into how to procure discounted copies for the boss of a small language school. A phone call to Cambridge University Press establishes that any money saved will not justify the hassle involved in setting up an account. My boss is appreciative of my efforts. As recompense, she gives me an old collection of teaching manuals which I now need to return to the flat and dump before going out this evening with a flatmate to watch Atletico Madrid.

I walk through a district that isn't renowned for any 'red light' activities. From out of nowhere appear two blondes who strongly resemble each other. Their approach to business is incredibly brazen. Politeness isn't a good strategy, and I have to wrench myself away from clasping hands. The bag of books impedes my escape. I pull myself angrily clear while feeling nevertheless a guilty sense of titillation.

They remind me of the Smith sisters at school, blonde-haired, blue-eyed twins – but not identical on account of Tracey's fuller figure.

When Tracey wasn't kissing boys, she blew bubbles of gum. Her mouth tasted of it and there were complaints, so I kept it to myself that I liked kissing Tracey. I wasn't bothered by the synthetic fruit flavours or a sweet stained tongue. I found her prettier than Jenny, but received wisdom had it that one progressed from Tracey to her skinnier sister, a progression for which I felt no inclination.

They were in the same class as me for RE lessons that were held in a Portakabin. It comprised two spaces; the largest being where we received instruction in the affairs of the divine and a much smaller area that gave off a distinctive damp smell from the peg hung coats. The teacher would carry the textbooks into the cabin with an air of weary resignation. A deal had been struck early. Our behaviour was conspicuously unrowdy for an RE class and guaranteed to remain so in return for a minimal line of inquiry and only nominal homework assignments.

It was among the coats that we learned to kiss during the three minutes of unsupervised time that separated RE and Maths; Miss Jenkins swiftly leaving the classroom as we reached out to our partners.

The Morgan Evans Auction Centre, Gaerwen, April 2004

This is my first visit to Morgan Evans and I'm a little disconcerted to see the cattle, trucks and pens. They may hold livestock auctions but it isn't my intention to leave with an actual lamb. A Charles Lamb maybe....

The salesroom, resembling a large warehouse, is where the 'Household' auction starts in twenty minutes. Fortunately there aren't many book lots to assess. A single box grabs my attention for it contains hundreds of Ladybird titles, their trademark logo and book format instantly recognisable.

Wills & Hepworth produced the first Ladybird book during the First World War, but it was in 1940 that the familiar pocket-sized Ladybird saw the light of day. I haven't time to examine all the books but I catch sight of a few titles that look promising – old enough to be originals in the animal series – like *Downy Duckling*. Some have dust jackets, which means they predate 1964.

My eight-pound bid, a modest enough sum, allows me to take home the box, which turns into a font of reminiscence.

There is a complete key word series of Peter and Jane titles, which helped me, along with thousands of children, to read. And I derive in an inordinate amount of pleasure from seeing a good number of their history titles: Sir Walter Raleigh, Oliver Cromwell, Robert the Bruce, David Livingstone, Captain Scott and my favourite, William the Conqueror. The cover has William on horseback, his arm raised to acknowledge the soldiers who surround him. My six-year-old ego associates itself with a conqueror. I envisage myself kneeling on the beach: 'In landing, he/I tripped and fell. For his/my followers this was a bad sign, but he/I stood up with both hands full of sand and earth.' Look,' he/I said. 'I have seized England with my two hands.' Pronouns merge as history melts into fantasy.

My grasp of history even today has its foundation in the reading of, and having read to me, Ladybird History books. The lives of famous people and events condensed expertly into Ladybird chunk sizes. And whole page colour illustrations to boot. The diversity of the subject matter hints at the vastness of it all and how it works: cars, trees, the human body, stamp collecting, etc. Knowledge imparted, not in a dry sense but calculated to invoke wonder. And all for 2/6 Net (2 shillings and sixpence), its monetary price, marked on the front end paper, kept fixed for some thirty years. The secret to its affordable pricing? Cleverly using a 56 page standardised format that was made from just one sheet size measuring 40 inches by 30 inches.

I can sell some titles for considerably more than 2/6. The series What to Look For: in Spring, Summer, Autumn and Winter, all illustrated by C. F. Tunnicliffe, always shift. But the discrepancy in prices between Ladybird books is difficult at times to fathom.

See below:

Item: The Story of Napoleon (A Ladybird 'Adventure from History' Book) by Peach, L...
Listing ID: 1111B677068
Purchased on: 2008-12-11
Postage Credit: £2.75
Buyer's Price: £0.01

Item: Tootles the Taxi and Other Rhymes by Joyce Blaikie Clegg; John Kenney
Listing ID: 1111K102601
Purchased on: 2008-11-30
Postage Credit: £2.75
Buyer's Price: £18.00

Phone Call to a Bookshop in Hay-on-Wye, 1992

Enquiring into the value of some Victorian magazines, a friendly voice says: 'Remember we never really own them, we are only custodians until somebody else takes over the job.'

Mind Travel, December 2006

Tipped off by my uncle that a bookshop in Palma is selling its entire stock, I make tentative enquiries. Being an itinerant bookseller allows me to dream of journeys actually taken, and to imagine others. Majorca's major city can be reached by taking a ferry from Sète. Could an inspection of the books justify the trip?

I exchange emails with Joachim who is handling the sale.

He sends me a 'books for sale' list as an Excel document. On it are some tantalising names. Robert Graves, as you might expect given his connections to Majorca, first editions of Allan Ginsberg's *Howl* and much more besides. All in all, a mouth-watering list of collectable authors but at a bank busting price; the total in excess of sixty thousand euros.

I soon gather that Joachim is acting on behalf of Simon Finch, a London book dealer based in Mayfair. Having recently paid £2.8 million for a 1623 First Folio edition of Shakespeare's plays, he might well be drumming up funds. These books in Majorca appear overvalued and Joachim agrees to some stringent price-cutting.

On 18 Dececember 2006, at 08:33, Joachim Reuter writes:

Hi Bill,

Sorry to insist so much after having taken a while to get back to you, but please let me know whether you are still interested in the books. As we are closing down before the end of the year, I need to know where to ship which books. If you are interested, we need to come to an agreement this week. As I mentioned in my last email the final price is negotiable beyond the 40% discount. So, please let me know your thoughts by tomorrow morning. If you want to reach me on my mobile today I am available all day.

Thanks
Best
Joachim

I'll have to pass. Sorry but I can't allow myself to be rushed into such a deal. I would be seriously interested if we are talking more along the lines of an 80% discount. (I consider the books to be very much overpriced) Otherwise I can't see any real margin in it for me.

There is no further contact.

The Road to Bangor Pier, April 2004

It's on the front page of the *Chronicle*, with Dan extolling its virtues along with those of the local land and seascape. A bookshop on Bangor Pier; the smallest in the world. And Dan's big claims don't end there. 'The most beautiful place to have a bookshop', he adds. It is.

A Victorian octagonal kiosk with an onion domed roof stands at the pier's entrance. Plywood shelves are diligently fitted. We fill them with a range of second-hand and new guidebooks and maps, those being supplied by Dan. It's a joint business venture/gimmick; Dan is using the kiosk to advertise his bookshop in the High Street and I am hoping to generate some buying opportunities.

We endeavour to keep the shop open at the weekends, weather permitting. A peppercorn rent charged by the council means that the kiosk doesn't need to be open on weekdays, when we are otherwise busy. And there are a few sunny Sundays. Dan brings along his deck chair based on the original 1935 Penguin book jacket design for *The Big Sleep*. We take turns in it; relishing a lounge with the Sunday papers. There are even customers to disturb our peace. On colder windy days it is, however, an effort to man the shop; our vigil fortified by tea and scones, courtesy of Vic and Sheila's tearoom at the far end of the pier. My daughter Emily keeps me company. Finding activities to alleviate her boredom and mine, we fly kites with difficulty, and catch crabs, even the occasional edible one, but they are too small to actually eat.

My fishing line is soon wetted; feathery lures hurled out into the strait to entice the mackerel; the sighting of whitebait giving us encouragement. Anne is missing her fresh fish. (It will be another three years before I take home freshly line caught bass, exchanged for books on the world art of tattoo.) Bait in the water, bait in the kiosk. Angling is an apt analogy for what I do. In casting from the pier, care is needed to avoid the jetty. Ah, the jetty. On the pier's east side. Grade II listed, I'll have you know. I know because I get it listed – this resilient narrow stone jetty, some 100 metres in length, sloping downward to the strait. Seaweed adheres to its roughly coursed stonework and the large blocks that form its surface. History resides in its architecture. And poetry too.

The jetty was marked as a pier on the 1831 Ordnance Survey map of the area, and is probably the site of an early crossing point to Anglesey. Garth Ferry was an important crossing point before the construction of the Menai Bridge in 1826. A ferry continued to operate from this jetty until the 1960s. I am given to ruminating on the jetty. Before long, I'm fantasising of re-establishing a ferry service between Garth Jetty and Beaumaris. I know a man with a boat licensed to carry passengers. But the council is decidedly unenthusiastic. You can only fantasise so much. Dan and I decide not to renew the lease.

A week preceding the kiosk's closure, a young woman asks me for 'that poem in the *Four Weddings and a Funeral* film.' Having no Auden in the kiosk I give her directions to Dan's shop.

The pier has an awe-inspiring panorama of wave, wood and mountain. Fixed to the benches are memorial plaques with touching inscriptions. 'In loving memory Florence Magdalen Feasy who swam the Menai Strait in 1929, aged 15'. 'Capt Marcel Le Comte 1938–2007 A true Garth boy Son of Henri and Gladys.'

Wind whistling through the shrouds in the boat yard is good for the lamentation of the soul. And for sheer power nothing beats Gruffudd ab yr Ynad Coch's Lament for Llywelyn ap Gruffudd, the last Prince.

'The heart's gone cold, under a breast of fear;
Lust shrivels like dried brushwood.
See you not the way of the wind and the rain?
See you not oaktrees buffet together?
See you not the sea stinging the land?
See you not truth in travail?
See you not the sun hurtling through the sky?
And that the stars are fallen?
Do you not believe God, demented mortals?
Do you not see the whole world's danger?
Why, oh my God, does the sea not cover the land?
Why are we left to linger?

Prades, Pyrenees, 1995

We drive to the Pyrenees via Carcassonne. Consuming several cloves of garlic in a cassoulet there has undesirable consequences. In the night the garlic will seep out from my every pore, much to everyone's disgust. Fortunately, by the time we call on a newsagent in Prades, a small town perched high in the Pyrenees, my body hasn't yet worked out a purging strategy for garlic overdose. It might have undermined the business proposal.

I have compiled a 200-book collection of holiday reads; best sellers in the main, including plenty of thrillers. The newsagent is open-minded; perfectly willing to take the books on sale or return basis. We agree to go halves on a standardised sale price of three francs.

Two weeks later I descend the Pyrenees, from near the Spanish border, on a little yellow train in an open-air carriage. We pass through little villages clinging to the rocky hillside, narrow gorges and tiny valleys. This scenic narrow gauge *petit train jaune* connects with a standard gauge service at Villefranche, the terminus for main-line trains from Perpignan. En route, I call on the Prades newsagent to learn that she has sold 108 books. In addition to English tourists, she tells me that Dutch and Germans are also buying.

Correze, November 1996

We take turns driving to Correze in a hired van. Brian, my new business partner, is in good form; his conversation is a strange mix of the sublime and the obscene. Brian's true passion is classical music and much of the four-hour journey is spent with Bach. We make appreciative sighs as the landscape rushes by until we venture up the driveway to a large farmhouse. Waiting to greet us is a self-described American aesthete and owner of one of the rare, complete sets of John James Audubon's *Birds of America*. I break the news that I don't have the confidence or contacts to handle his piece de resistance or his facsimile reproduction of the Leonardo da Vinci notebooks and Codices. I offer to buy his First Edition of Chatwin's *In Patagonia* but he is reluctant to accept less than £250 for it. We agree, however, to a price on the paperbacks; a one thousand strong collection of modern literature, in tip top condition, in which there is a fair sprinkling of cult titles and books with a high 'novelty' factor (always a big plus) like Dennis Cooper's George Miles cycle.

Having come prepared, we soon begin the labour intensive process of packing the boxes. Overweight and in his fifties, Brian isn't the fittest of individuals. He sweats heavily while helping me lug the boxes into the van.

'You're the muscle, eh?' says the American who has emerged from the kitchen with coffee.

What I imagine to be a wry smile escapes my lips. Oxbridge graduate and former Head of English at Exeter College, Brian now organises poetry recitals in the shop when he isn't leading a choir in the Cathedral of Beziers, a city to where he supposedly retired. An accomplished pianist, Brian is also something of an artist when it comes to performing lengthy monologues on a myriad of intellectual topics. The American is treated to one on rhythmic patterns in English and French classical music

'Well, well. You're the most intellectual muscle I've ever come across.'

We leave in a van which, with all its book ballast, now feels easier to handle as we begin the long drive back.

Moving to 44 Rue de l'Université, Montpellier, 1996

The opening of a sex shop next door in rue de Cheval Vert was not our prime reason for moving. Nor was it a reason to stay put. We had been looking for a bigger place.

The owners of a shop, selling new books at the top of the street we've moved to, feel threatened by our sudden presence, but we are ignoring their enmity. I won't be turning down textbook orders but I'm not chasing the student market in spite of our new address. We're attracted to a different concept, more of an ideal actually, one encompassing tea, cake and a good read. 'BBC', in moving from rue de Cheval Vert to rue l'Université, has opened an adjoining tea-room. These days every business refers to a pretentious mission statement. If we had one, ours would be based on the following paragraph from Carson McCullers' *The Ballad of the Sad Cafe*.

> 'But the spirit of a café is altogether different. Even the richest, greediest old rascal will behave himself, insulting no one in a proper café. And poor people look about them gratefully and pinch up the salt in a dainty and modest manner. For the atmosphere of a proper café implies these qualities: fellowship, the satisfaction of the belly, and a certain gaiety and grace of behaviour.'

We tempt shoppers with scones, melting moments and bara brith. But our business model is flawed. Many customers turn into friends and it's difficult to refuse them a tea or a scone on the house.

All sorts of people walk into the shop with a multitude of motives other than wanting a good read. In six months, I encounter clowns, buskers, beggars, thieves, novelists (Adam Thorpe, Sam David), poets, pavement artists, aspirant suicides (I have to pretend that I no longer have a copy of the *Handbook of Hanging*) and replica gun-toting junkies.

A tall Yorkshireman with an eyepatch, who is rumoured to be on the run, steps into shop on the look out 'for a dirty old man'. He pauses for effect before adding: 'Charles Bukowski'. I don't have any because Bukowski is an author that flies off the shelves. It transpires that Bob really is a wanted man. Amenable, and an avid reader of literature, his presence bothers nobody in the shop, least of all me. Eventually caught by police at Montpellier train station, he is extradited back to Britain from where his solicitor contacts me to request a character reference. I willingly comply. There is mention at a Parole Tribunal of a now banned medicine once used for treating epilepsy and Bob is soon released.

Lecturers and authors breach the shop's entrance but I find myself more intrigued by the conversations I have with society's more disaffected members.

Hailing originally from Ladbroke Grove, Tony the tramp has been eking out a beggar's existence for at least a decade in southern France. A diminutive, handsome man, Tony has lived with the gypsies but is now a confirmed inhabitant of the streets. He confesses to having stolen books from outside my first shop but I can't muster any real anger such is his likeable demeanour, providing he's not too far gone on wine. We lend pens and help to compose heartrending slogans, on pieces of cardboard, designed to elicit sympathy and cash. Anne gives Tony soup and he genuinely wants to help our fortunes;

offering to distribute flyers about the town. One day he is excited because Motörhead are in town. Tony intends to beg a guitar off Lemmy, a former friend, but he misses the concert because of an exceptionally drunken binge.

There are people who believe my working in an English bookshop is proof of an allegiance to all things English, exclusively so. I am required on occasion to point out that the shop contains just as many American authors. And also helping to fill the shelves are plenty of books by Welsh, Irish and Scottish writers.

A great deal of social intercourse is involved in running the shop. Sometimes it is welcome, but there are days when you lose the will to haul up the shop shutters. Montpellier is an increasingly popular destination for English speaking holiday-makers. I give them a potted history of the city, extolling its attributes and warning them about its high petty crime rate. Some express their thanks and buy the guidebook recommended at the end of my spiel. But I grow quickly wary of the tourists who monopolise my time before deciding that they have quite enough 'reading material' on them. So why walk into a bookshop? The tourist board would more usefully employ me. I begin to recognise the signs that betray a determined non-buyer. Overly effusive in their praise of the city, they merely want to communicate this fact with someone who speaks their language. I develop a tactic to uncover some paperwork requiring my urgent attention. This doesn't always work though and I can find myself trapped, longing to escape. One spring morning a softly spoken Canadian walks into the shop, introducing himself as 'Don Bell, book scout.' He has difficulty breathing but manages to convey his intriguing life style; that of cruising the bookshops and flea markets in Paris.

Our conversation makes me hanker for the open road. I recognise a fellow spirit but learn only after out meeting that he wrote a book, *Saturday Night at the Bagel Factory*, that won the 1973 Stephen Leacock Memorial Medal for humour.

Prague, February 1996

The air is cold but invigorating. I'm staying with my brother and his Czech girlfriend who live here. I knew that Czechs were big on beer but their penchant for ice cream has come as a surprise.

Tom and Katka give me a potted tour of the city before taking me to the Globe Bookstore. It exudes a welcoming atmosphere (all the buildings in this city seem to have a surplus of heat) and they serve hot food as well as cakes. I note the international newspapers and permit myself a quick scan of the books whose prices are higher than I expected. A friend tells me of someone who buys second-hand books in bulk from charity book depots to sell to shops throughout Europe. As you head east the prices increase.

Drinking strong coffee, we overhear a good-natured argument over Czechoslovakian literature. A group of Americans debate whether either Franz Kafka or Milan Kundera can be considered as Czech writers. Neither author wrote in Czech, they contend, before an irritated Czech pipes up to question their hegemony of opinion.

We leave the Globe and head out for more traditional tourist destinations. I have a fleeting impression that all in Prague is bars and bookshops. The atmosphere is suitably bohemian.

Agde, South of France, June 1996

Agde is a town on the Herault river about a mile inland from the Mediterranean, to the south-west of the Etang de Thau. It is sometimes known as 'The Black Pearl of the Mediterranean' because of the dark colour of the volcanic rock used in many of its buildings. In one of the town's winding, narrow streets is a garage full of English books. They are all for sale, belonging to a former diplomat, or so I am told by Gerald, a member of Agde's ex-pat community, who has tipped me off. Gerald has also hinted at the man's mysterious past.

After I rendezvous with Gerald in Agde, he takes me to a small house where I am introduced to an elegant man in his eighties called John. Before talking business, I am invited to sit in the kitchen where Gerald is instructed to serve us all a glass of chilled red wine. It is a good antidote to the heat of an Agde summer. John is proud of, and keen to share, his recent discovery of keeping red wine in the fridge. He seems on friendly terms with Gerald who is enjoying his drink. They both enjoy each other's company.

Too frail to accompany me to the garage, John leaves me alone to gauge his library, which consists, in the main, of the crime, thriller and spy genres. At a rough count, there are more than a thousand.

I return to the kitchen where he is more than happy to accept an offer of 3000 francs. 'Is that too much?' he asks. I find myself shaking my head. 'No. No. It's fair.' What's happening to my negotiating skills? Am I being hypnotised by a diplomat's charm?

Gerald kindly helps me load this massive library of paperbacks into the Renault 5. It takes an age. John is amazed when we fit all the books in. Some spill over the gear stick and into the drivers' footwell. Among the books is a sprinkling of classics, some being novels by Dickens whom, I am informed by John, the Russians revered. While based in Moscow, John learned that the Russians considered Charles Dickens to be a chronicler of the evils of capitalism. John is ready to reminisce further but I need to be making tracks.

Driving back to Montpellier I'm feeling good. Surrounded by so many books, it reminds me of the Ales' haul; a sea of Deightons and Le Carres rising up from the seats to obscure the view out of the back window. I find it difficult to focus. Poetry can be a dangerous thing too, it's distracting me from the business of driving. Out of the corner of my eye, I can make out early editions of Auden and T. S. Eliot's *The Four Quartets* in pamphlet form. At the traffic lights, a quick rummage turns up *The Poetics of Rilke*, an early translation. I catch the bemused expressions on the faces of nearby motorists.

Fighting the urge to look further, I arrive home safely. After an hour of heavy labour, the books form a jumbled pile on the sitting room floor. I love the business of rooting through them; looking out for good reads (a subjective choice, obviously) and the rarities to be sold for a handsome profit.

Catching the eye is The Fantastiks, W. S. Scott's selection of writers (Donne, Herbert, Crashaw, Vaughan) of metaphysical verse. Highlighted is the poem: 'To his Mistris going to bed'.

'Come, madam, come, all rest my powers defie;
Until I labour, I in labour lie.
The foe oft-times, having the foe in sight,
Is tir'd with standing, though he never fight.
Off with that girdle, like heaven's Zone glittering,

But a far fairer world encompassing.
Unpin that spangled breast-plate that you wear,
That th' eyes of busie fooless may be stopt there.'

It is a guilt-tinged pleasure to go through someone's collection of books; a kind of invasion of privacy. There are dedications to, and from, wives and lovers and friends. School prizes for promising compositions. Going by the books' contents and inscriptions within, a person's life and their interests can be loosely pieced together.

John's copy of *The Scottish Songbook* was presented to him at Harrow. There are references in other books to time spent in Cambridge as a student. His profile wouldn't be out of place in the milieu of Kim Philby et al. Is this why Gerald had talked of spooks?

Pink Floyd at Domaine De Grammont, Montpellier, August 1994

We are on the outskirts of a park at dusk on the eastern side of Montpellier. Pink Floyd will be taking to the stage in about an hour. The crowd is making its way to the entrance of an open-air leisure centre.

Mum has come along to give moral support. Mixing with the ticket touts, we are attempting to shift ten copies of a book on Pink Floyd. A Penguin rep. has palmed off them on me as sure sellers, exploiting my enthusiasm for the band.

The books, published to coincide with the group's The Division Bell Tour, have failed to sell in my shop; and the concertgoers are showing a singular lack of interest in them despite of my best efforts at impersonating a cockney wide boy. We slash our prices as my desperation shows but this seems to repel any potential buyers. The English touts aren't having any more luck. The consensus among them is that the French find their activities an alien concept, that of fly by night transactions.

It's a relief to give up upon hearing the strains of 'Astronomy Domine' that signal the concert's start. 'Lime and limpid green, a second scene. A fight between the blue you once knew. Floating down, the sound resounds...'

Going to our car, I make out the tune 'Money' from *The Dark Side of the Moon*, which was one the first albums I bought. The irony is not lost on me.

Teddington Lock, 1974

It writhes in agony and I let it take the line out towards the pillar in the middle of the river. It disappears from sight. Nobody would have known that beneath that placid surface a creature is swimming in great pain. We have been unable to extricate the hook from its throat.

Eddy calls for its execution. I agree, reeling in the eel. I have Eddy's French flick knife at the ready. The sun is shining, but the blade doesn't glisten. Eddy wedges the eel tight against a rock with his trainer. Then I take the knife and without hesitation shove the blade into the eel's gill opening. The flesh is soft and cuts easily. But then the knife meets more resistance. By vigorously sawing, the eel's throat is sliced apart. My hand slips off the knife's handle, which remains projecting out from the eel. The rock turns crimson. Eddy watches on in morbid curiosity as I pull the knife free. The eel is still now. The wind has dropped. 'Bloody hell,' says Eddy. We take it to show Mike.

Out it flops with a heavy thud. The head of an eel bearing prominent blood orange eyes with coal black pupils. Rigor mortis has set in, jamming shut the beak-like mouth. The body of the eel is slow to emerge but its hugeness is quickly apparent. The stratification of colour became more distinct towards its tail; a greenish brown top which contrasts with an anaemic yellow underbelly.

We think the creature alien; an atavistic vision sliding out from a bag before our very eyes. Impeding a smooth exit are the eel's pectoral fins which catch around the edges of the bag. Then it is fully exposed, more than three feet in length. The thickest part of its girth is the size of a man's clenched fist.

Eddy is irritated to see me with a book in hand. It's the *Observer's Book of Coarse Fishing*. I soon find the eel in question. The common eel (*Anguilla anguilla*), but ours is uncommonly large.

Years later, I will buy other editions in considerably better condition. My edition as a boy would have tempted few buyers: *Wheat, Peter. Illustrated by East, Baz. Frederick Warne. 1977. Observer book no. 59. 8 colour plates, 18 b/w photos. Damp marks to bottom edge of boards and badly torn wrapper missing pieces. Muddy fingerprints on most pages.*

* The *Observer* books are collectible, especially those with high numbers. I recently sold the *Observer's Book on Paris (1st Edition 1982, Book is in v. good con., no inscriptions, marks or tears. Front and rear boards are bright and white and corners are sharp and square, spine is unfaded)* for £70.

Top deck 281, Twickenham Green, 1978

From the top deck of the bus, I see people, with beer-induced hunger, congregating outside gaudily lit take-aways. Head against glass, I catch sight of my features coarsened somehow by the sombre reflection of them. I had wanted to discuss cosmetic surgery with my doctor but I chickened out when I saw that his nose was bigger than mine. But is my mug more ugly/interesting than ugly/plain? A passage in the *The Catcher in the Rye* draws a distinction between boys who are classically good looking and boys who are attractive in an interesting way. The book's protagonist Holden Caulfield gets me thinking. Could I be ugly in an interesting way? I am almost the same age as Holden. My enthusiasm for the book rubs off on Eddy. We go into a bookshop to locate a copy. It's equivalent to six Double Decker chocolate bars (complete with the accompanying Willie Rushton impressions) but Eddy buys it nonetheless. I recall the awe felt by my teenage self for how certain writers render experience into believable worlds.

Pipe dreaming in Nîmes 1991

Living off the proceeds from some good sales (including the Virginia Woolf), I am killing time with Marmite. We meet in the bar at the Youth Hostel. Being English and six foot five, Marmite stands out. A student at l'Ecole Supérieure des Beaux-Arts de Nîmes, Marmite is in between lodgings. And I am, in a sense, in between books.

We drink on average two bottles of rosé a day when we're

not high on dope. Marmite feels this is good preparation for his work as an artist. Attendance at the art school is not compulsory so we are both able to while away our afternoons amid the marble sculptures in the Jardin de la Fontaine. Marmite has an appetite for Byron and reflecting on matters of a philosophical nature, while I have a natural tendency to daydream. Marmite is also heavily into Sartre. (I doubt you could ever say that the other way round. Once, being overtaken on the M42 by a van in the shape of giant Marmite jar, the existential gloom of being stuck on a motorway lifts suddenly.)

Lounging with lizards, we observe the tourists making their way up the hill on a stone stairway to the Tour Magne. Built by Augustus in 15 BC, the Tour Magne was originally part of the ramparts encircling the city. Bathed in light at night, this ancient block of stone takes on a magical appearance. It overlooks Nîmes where there is a remarkably intact amphitheatre. These days it is the bulls of the Camargue, rather than gladiators, who face slaughter inside it. Behind a large ornate gate, the tranquil confines of the gardens are, of course, closeted from the real world. Elderly locals sit and play cards. We admire such lethargy and take our cue from them. Marmite and I rarely reach the Tour Magne; our half-hearted ascents taking us no further than a small pond fed by a tiny waterfall. At the pool's edge is a covering of lightly splashed grass upon which we sit, and peer in.

'I always thought of you as being into pond life,' Marmite says. Red worms wriggle below surface-skating insects. And there are tadpoles, those black fleshy commas, that make me remember meat string dangled into the class aquarium at primary school for them to feast upon. Mason Lilly used to delight us by fishing them out to eat. He'd trained on worms picked from the school's sports field.

A small girl in a red dress distracts me from my reverie. In approaching the pool, she spots an inert tadpole stranded on the grassy verge. '*Il est mort*,' she declares. But after dropping the tadpole in the water, she excitedly announces its resurrection. '*Il est vivant*.' Her father smiles.

On most days in the gardens, we rarely make it as far as the pond. For we are becoming pétanque aficionados. Nicely stoned, we sit and watch the games that are played out in place Pablo Picasso. Pétanque is a form of boules where the aim (no pun intended) is, while standing with the feet together in a small circle, to throw hollow metal balls as close as possible to a small wooden ball, red in colour, called a *cochonnet* (jack). Other objects, for more impromptu games, are also used such as car keys.

They play every day after lunch upon a triangular patch of chalky ground which is Nîmes' designated boulodrome. Sturdy sweet chestnut branches provide shade, increasingly so, as the weeks pass, with the development of the trees' leaves and glove-like fruits. Place Picasso's elite band of players comprise the bellyman and three others, all of whom we label as potential Mr Men characters for yet more books by Roger Hargreaves.

Scarcely visible below a black beret are telltale strands of whitening hair. His mouth, in contrast, is tenderly defined, resembling a child's, but it isn't really his face that captures our attention. To us, he is the 'bellyman'. For he has a fine big belly which means that his back is straighter that the others when he crouches to throw. The cockiness of his spirit is familiar and pleasing to the spectators who habitually line both sides of his corridor of play. Visiting the Jardin de la Fontaine for the first time, even we, as novice spectators, cannot fail to see that the bellyman is the most accomplished of players. His prize possession is that of an easy swinging left arm that delivers a boule with enviable consistency.

For a man in his forties the 'wigman' is slim and agile, but the wig dupes few; its jet-blackness clashing with its wearer's anaemic complexion. The wigman specialises in knocking his adversary's boules to a safe non-point scoring distance from the jack. He also has a penchant for directing the jack towards the trunks of trees and their surrounding roots, thereby diluting the game's skill factor. Above the trees' knobbly bases, the bark has patches coloured white by the esplanade's dust and earth. We derive a simple pleasure from watching the dust lift into the limpid air as a result of a boule's emphatic descent. The bellyman copes with any sort of terrain; little troubling the lucid swing of his muscular arm. It has an air of roughness about it, a naturalness that is raw and unpretentious. There is also his laugh, a deep-throated explosion of goodwill. And accompanying cries of *merde* and *putain*, expletives rarely prompted by self-error. More likely a partner has strayed with a boule.

Rue Dorée is one of Nîmes' quieter streets that seems permanently in shadow. Halfway along it is a small English centre where a middle-aged American woman sells teaching materials and some fiction. I buy a Penguin copy of *The Red and the Black* by Stendhal and become unhealthily obsessed by its central character, Julien Sorel, who has a young man's ambition to become successful in the aristocratic society of 1830s France. Julien's change of appearance, alternating between the uniform of the army and the church, between the red and the black, is symbolic of the conflict in his personality between truthfulness and pretence. It's probably due to a diet of cannabis, wine and almond croissants, but reading the book gives rise to some pretty deluded ideas. A recurring one is to join the Foreign Legion. I don't even need to run off to do it because there is an Infantry Regiment based in Nîmes. Marmite is sceptical and says he can't see me in the uniform. He is soon sharing a studio flat with another 'artist' at the school. I decline an offer to flat share since I like the sense of impermanence that the hostel gives me; an illusion of unplanned adventure. It also provides a good cheap meal in the evening. We still meet regularly in the gardens. Marmite starts to talk of art instead of philosophy. His fellow students' work is too abstract for my taste but I keep a diplomatic silence. There is endless talk about Pierre's tank sculptures that are exciting the lecturers. I am invited to parties where Marmite and I are something of a novelty. Marmite's promiscuous nature (both social and sexual) is given free reign. I don't share his success with the girls, although Sandrine and her friends are tolerant of my tentative efforts to communicate in French. When my timidity isn't taken for rudeness, I enjoy the evenings spent at the Salon Vert. The students soon allow me to park the Princess in the grounds of the art school; the caretaker doesn't seem to mind. Marmite and I go for occasional trips to the sea, taking water with us for when the car inevitably overheats. These trips are meant to be hangover cures. I blame Marmite for his fixation with Byron.

> 'Man, being reasonable, must get drunk,
> the best of life is but intoxication:
> Glory, the grape, love, gold, in these are sunk,
> The hopes of all men, and every nation;

Without their sap, how branchless were the trunk
Of life's strange tree, so fruitful on occasion.'

I walk alongside the canals populated by swans and ducks. Swimming to avoid blooms of algae, these balls of living thread give purpose to the birds' movements. They make me think about my current lack of direction. It is weeks since I have been book hunting. Marmite has an idea. To put up an ad – 'We buy English books/On achete livres en anglais' – in the Le Sémaphore cinema where English films are regularly shown *en version originale*. There is no immediate response but the initiative serves to assuage the guilt arising from a Protestant work ethic that lingers despite attempts to kill it off.

Minutes before arriving at the boulodrome, I hear the collective hum of conversations punctuated by the clink of pastis-filled glasses. Marmite is already in position, spliff in hand, doing a convincing impression of Withnail. He points out the 'young pretender'. Too young as yet to convincingly pretend, his skills might one day mount a credible challenge to the bellyman. He already has the measure of the wigman who resorts to his chief spoiling tactic by putting the jack in the vicinity of the trees. This does not unsettle the young pretender now he has hit form. But the young pretender lacks consistency and Marmite questions his temperament. A silver ring in his left ear glints in the sun, catching the eye as does the young man's easiness of carriage and gesture. Endowed with charisma, he has a cigarette perpetually on the go. It releases into the fresh but warming days of April, plumes of pungent Gitane smoke.

On most days the 'flashman' is the fourth member. On late Tuesdays and even later Thursdays, however, a thin man, with a gentle arm action, participates by default, stepping into the bellyman's illustrious corridor of play. There is a price to pay for his flashiness, namely a job, one requiring his attendance elsewhere. It enables him to arrive at place Picasso in a Porsche, out from which he swaggers, clad in Armani. When present at the boulodrome, he lacks nothing in dedication. His costly garb captures the dirt and dust when he curls himself up into a human ball. A rapid upright movement then brings about the release of the boule. His skills, though considerable, are not given sufficient time to be honed. Before departing for work the 'flashman' gives the boules a thorough clean before attending to his own appearance. He keeps a tin of brown shoe polish in the boot of the Porsche.

It is a most civilised way of whiling away an afternoon; an indulgence really, like the mixing of Pernod and water. We are utterly seduced by this ambience of lazy talk and cigarettes. This state of torpor, it lasts until the jack bounces unexpectedly close to the bank of spectators. A melodramatic rush of activity then ensues; people shuffling back, others having to extricate themselves from chairs. The boules also, on occasion, whizz through the air like cannons. Missing their target (a boule needing to be dislodged), they then scatter spectators in all directions.

The Mairie and everyone at the art school are getting worked up about the imminent arrival of Julian Schnabel. New York's high priest of abstract art will be making an appearance at the Musee des Beaux-Arts for the *vernisage*. Marmite explains that this is like a private preview-cum-party to mark the start of an art exhibition. He gives me an invitation.

What first strikes me about the paintings are their huge

size (twenty-two-foot-square paintings) and all the crucifixes on show. I don't really get it. Marmite is more analytical and says Schnabel's success is a natural evolution of the art scene, as predicted by Tom Wolfe's *The Painted Word*, a book Marmite finds in the English centre. It concludes that modern art has become as academic and as cliquey as the salon painting against which it first rebelled. Marmite isn't wholeheartedly in agreement. He, after all, has to make his way in this world.

I fail to decipher the Schnabel art on show, finding it painful, almost, to behold. There is adequate compensation though: delicious canapés and champagne, courtesy of the Mairie's largesse. I don't hang around long enough to catch a glimpse of Schnabel but I do get to meet an art student called Anne.

The exhibition ends three weeks later but three of Schnabel's works are left to grace the walls of the Maison Carrée, a well preserved temple built in the first century bc and dedicated to Lucius and Caius Caesar, grandsons of the Emperor. This is an irritant to us because every time we walk back to Marmite's flat after a pétanque session, we pass the temple and are reminded of the Emperor's new clothes inside.

Marmite has begun sketching the boules players. We keenly observe their idiosyncracies. The bellyman displays fewer than the others, preferring to spend as little time as possible in sizing up his throw. When presented with a throw requiring a fine judgement, he plucks from his back pocket a handkerchief into which he noiselessly blows his fat nose. Slow in settling down to throw, the wigman tends to pace up and down the corridor of play before remarking the throwing circle by scraping his shoes hard and repeatedly into the ground. After badly misjudging a throw he is inclined to go through the motions with an imaginary boule, rectifying the error in his mind if not in reality. In spite of his tender years, the young pretender has already acquired several habits; energetically hitching up his jeans in a general air of self-exhortation to perform well, then banging the ground with the boules before knocking them against each other as though putting them through a test of loyalty. The flashman, we joyfully note, likes to juggle with his.

The largest crowd gathers for the bellyman. But other pétanque players, despite carrying less esteem, also have their followers. The standard of play is variable, especially when it is friendship, as opposed to ability or generation that binds the participants together in competition. Age has modified the stance of some competitors. For those with stiffened arthritic backs, magnets, discreetly carried in pockets, are lowered on elastic to retrieve the boules. Marmite wonders if a good toke on his joint might further alleviate their discomfort.

With the afternoon's games finally on the wane, I part company with Marmite to see how the tadpoles are faring. Eminently watchable, their food attacks are carnivorous and candid. Impatient children, seeking for proof of the promised transmogrification, don't have long to wait. Limbs appear, tails shrink and a new creature is formed.

It happens while Anne and I are making plans to leave Nîmes. Marmite witnesses it before me. Everyone finds it hard to believe. The bellyman losing his touch? Concentration knots his facial features into an expression of unwavering determination. But his adversaries, in sensing unprecedented fallibility, gang up. The wigman scores victories without placing the jack in the bumpier regions. The young pretender is less inhibited. The flashman postpones his time of departure for work. They become aware of the bellyman's struggle to hold his own when the jack is thrown out far from their feet, a tactic to put uncertainty into his mind.

I can't help but feel bad for the bellyman but Marmite is largely indifferent to his declining talent. The chirpy self-assurance is going. Ripples of both empathy and discontentment run among supporters who have basked in his parochial glory. Some have even won money by betting on him. He experiments with his action, not crouching so low to the ground. But then his belly becomes a hindrance rather than a help – no longer helping to achieve an equilibrium of body. This new posture doesn't lend itself to boules-throwing exactitude. In releasing the boule it is obvious that he is off balance, at risk even of toppling over to complete the humiliation. In cursing the boules, he tosses them higher into the air but altering their trajectory fails to work. Confusion and resentment widen the furrows upon his brow, along which run large beads of sweat. He employs acts of superstition that have previously ended barren spells. He rubs a yellow rag frenziedly against his hip. His nose is blown hard while he prolongs the time spent in terrain assessment, marking and remarking the grit in the throwing circle. He even appears to reduce his pastis intake. His mistakes cause increasing embarrassment. His rare victories are now due more to opponent error.

A man purporting to clear houses has phoned regarding the advertisement in the Le Sémaphore cinema. Marmite has taken the message, which is, broadly, that the man has a large number of English books that he wants rid of at a price to be established. I phone the man from Anne's flat and it turns out that the books are in Alès, a town lying lies 25 miles north-west of Nîmes, on the left bank of the Gardon River. At the risk of appearing too keen, I fix up a meeting for the following day. He gives me directions to a car park near to the town's centre.

I spot a white Renault Trafic van and pull up alongside. A man in his fifties jumps out at the sight of the Princess with its English plates. He wastes no time in yanking open the back doors to his van. The sight of hundreds of books greets me. It is often the case, upon being called out to inspect a library for sale, that the books will be all good or all bad. Within seconds I know that it hasn't been a wasted trip. Now I need to enter negotiating mode. I make a show of counting the books as my mind does the calculations. I see promising titles. How now to convey an impression of insouciance? You tend to do your best negotiating when you genuinely are prepared to walk away from the deal. But it's difficult to feign that frame of mind. Neither of us is keen to suggest a figure. I say, rather dishonestly, that as a general lot they're okay while adding, honestly, that I can't see any really rare items. '*Allez cinq cent francs,*' suggests the man. I nod, trying to keep a serious face.

The Austin Princess isn't the most stylish of vehicles but it has good cabin space that I put to full use. I love the smell and the jumbled piles of all these books; vast quantities of American Penguins and Vintage paperbacks, many of which have the name and address of their former owner stamped on the inside cover. Going by past experience, it won't hinder the selling of them.

The Princess is overheating again but it gets me and the books back to Nîmes. Lacking confidence to approach a garage, I can't continue to patch up its radiator. So the Princess ends its days in the grounds of the art school where the students make a sculpture out of it. Marmite keeps me informed but after completing his 'academic' year, we lose touch. We both stop the drinking; Marmite no longer convinced of alcohol's incantatory powers to produce good art.

Before leaving Nîmes, I visit the Jardin de la Fontaine one last time with Anne. I show her the pond where the tadpoles are moving with less hectic abandon; their tails having all but disappeared. May is warming the days. We pass by the boulodrome. I haven't witnessed the tadpoles's complete metamorphosis but in place Picasso there is a definite indicator of time passing. Still venting joy or frustration in his inimitable fashion, a rotund and familiar figure is engaged in a game of boules with a set of players I don't recognise.

Anne has quit art school and moved to Montpellier where I want to try my luck with the recent spoils from Alès. I take up residence in the city's youth hostel at the bottom of rue de l'Université. We have been told about a book market held on Saturday mornings under Les Arceaux, the city's ancient aqueduct. The project is to sell books there, out of the back of a van.

Pont de Montvert, Late August 1990

I've come down from Mount Lozère, passing near to where Robert Louis Stevenson had slept the night under the stars. Drinking a cool can of Coke on the humpbacked bridge (Pont-de-Montvert) that spans the swift-flowing Tarn, I feel an acute sense of well being. I've been following in the footsteps of the writer's 120-mile solo hiking journey through the sparsely populated areas of the Cévennes Mountains. Travelling without a donkey (just as well given that Stevenson's Modestine was a stubborn beast he could never quite get the better of), I'm now confident about completing the walk despite sore, blistered feet. It's my own fault, choosing to wear a black pair of Dr Martens that never properly fitted me. It's been cold in the tent at night and yet hot, very hot on some days after what was a distinctly inauspicious start, landing up at the wrong Le Monastier, some 150 km off course from Le Monastier-sur-Gazeille, where Stevenson actually began his walk.

At one end of the bridge is the tourist office, which has for sale a bilingual (English/French) edition of *Travels with a Donkey* with an unusually detailed map of Stevenson's route. I resist a strong impulse to buy it. My funds, after all, are running low.

On the bridge, I skim through my travel notes.

'Wrong bloody Le Monastier. Fool. Put right by an amused lady in the village's boulangerie, I venture, weeping with frustration, into a nearby church. Above its altar is a sign that has an implacable logic to it: *'La Route est Longue'*! Must now spend an unscheduled night in the train station in Le Mende, a town whose Cathedral is adorned with Gothic devil dogs carved in a permanent retch. I feel (and look) a bit like them after too much wine. – Return to La Bastide, couple of lifts, arrive in Le Monastier in heavy rain. Spot a commemorative plaque dedicated to Stevenson and his donkey. 'LE 22 SEPTEMBER 1878, ROBERT LOUIS STEVENSON POUR SON VOYAGE A TRAVERS LES CEVENNES AVEC UN ANE.' (I've left my Anne in Montpellier) –

Leave at noon. Punishing early ascent; ripped by thorns and a sad proliferation of barbed wire. 2.30 arrive in St

Martin de Frugeres. Exhilarating descent at 3.45. Arrive in Goudet. Blistered feet. The river, described by Stevenson as 'an amiable stripling of a river', is today at least 60 feet wide, teeming with dirty black trout. Icy cold to the touch. Fly fisherman tries his luck as the sun goes down behind the chateau Beaufort –

Very cold at night in the tent. Ussel 11.45 a.m. WWI memorial. Sweat stinging the eyes. Feet burning, try wearing espadrilles. Begin to revel in the surroundings but there remains, as Stevenson says, a lingering desire for a companion in travel. –

Le Bruchet 4p.m. stone walls dividing fields in which tractors and farm machinery lie abandoned. Directed to campsite, only me camping. Feels like I'm walking on hot coals – hope they cool sufficiently to allow me to continue to Pradelles. Next day, more drizzle. To the east green gently rolling hills. My water bottle swings to and thro', metronome like and making me aware of a fairly constant stride pattern. Pass Mount Fouey – phoeey 3600 feet, scarcely aware of the height – Limp into Pradelle at 5.45 p.m. Ensconced in sleeping bag for 12 hours, recovering from tiredness brought on my climb into town. It's damp & miserable so make it a rest day. Get out my books. Finish reading *The Bell Jar* and *Death of An Expert Witness*. In Langogne, deduce Allier to be much swollen by recent rainfall given the description of it by Stevenson. Beautiful descent into Le Cheylad L'Eveque. Plod on but climb Lozère with surprising ease.'

I look up from the notebook. Pont-de-Montvert has retained the stony granite-built traditional aspect of traditional villages in this part of the Cévennes. Stevenson writes that it is here that the repressive Abbé de Chayla lived – the 'Archpriest of the Cevennes' who sparked the rebellion of the Camisards. His house in Pont-de-Montvert served as a prison for Protestants who were tortured. As Stevenson recounts, Chayla 'closed the hands of his prisoners upon live coal, and plucked out the hairs of their beards, to convince them that they were deceived in their [religious beliefs].'

I look for signs of where the house might have stood before it was burnt down in July 1702 and the Abbé killed.

'One by one, Séguier first, the Camisards drew near and stabbed him. "This," they said, "is for my father broken on the wheel. This for my brother in the galleys. That for my mother or my sister imprisoned in your cursed convents." Each gave his blow and his reason; and then all kneeled and sang psalms around the body till the dawn. With the dawn, still singing, they defiled away towards Frugèresmap, farther up the Tarn, to pursue the work of vengeance, leaving Du Chayla's prison-house in ruins, and his body pierced with two-and-fifty wounds upon the public place.'

The subsequent Protestant rebellion was severely repressed by Louis XIV. I have a good feeling about this place that I can't explain. It's got nothing to do with its Protestant heritage for I have no affinity to any religion. It's pleasant also to be close to so much water in the heat of the day. The village was built at the confluence of the Tarn, Rieumalet and Martinet rivers, beside which is situated the municipal campsite. As is usual, the facilities are good. After showering I get into conversation with a German couple who are desperate for reading material. I give them the Sylvia Plath and the P. D. James but they insist on handing me 50 francs after I decline a beer from their camping van fridge. What is going on? This was a trip to take stock of my life but I've unintentionally become involved in a book deal of sorts.

I use the money to buy the bilingual edition of *Travels with a Donkey*.

(From *Clear Waters Rising* by N. Crane 'It wasn't until I read his journal that I realised he'd lopped off the end of this passage when he rewrote the text for TWAD. After "I travel for travel's sake," he added in the original: "And to write about it afterwards..."'

A Royal Customer, Bangor, November 2009

The book in my hand connects me to royalty, albeit tenuously. Laurie Lee's *The Firstborn* is illustrated with black and white photographs taken by the author. He wrote it while contemplating the future of his newborn child.

A few days following my birth in October 1964, my aunt gave my mother a copy of this book.

> 'This moment of meeting seemed to be a birthtime
> for both of us; her first and my second life.
> Nothing I knew would be the same again. She is of
> course just an ordinary miracle, but is also the late
> wonder of my life. So each night I take her to bed
> like a book and lie close and study her.'

Recently, I removed the book from the 'family, not for sale, I'll murder you if you do' shelf. It was given a description of its condition and edition (second impression) and put on sale through Amazon.

A member of the Royal Family has just purchased the book online.

Book Blindness, Twickenham, 1997

According to my database, the book is in the box labelled 'Strawberry Hill 22', which in another life contained Sainsbury bananas. I've been through boxes 21 and 23 and am now looking through box 22 for the third time. In my mind's eye the book resembles an Everyman's Library (Dent) small format hardback. I recheck my database. I recheck my invoices. No record of a sale. The book must be there. I make myself read out the title of every book and it is only then that I spot it. It's a bloody paperback.

Book blindness is a condition that afflicts all sellers at one time or other.

Travelling to Paris, 1989

Phil, friend and sub-editor, has presented me with a guidebook as a leaving present in which he has inscribed the following lines from a poem by Auden:

'Look, stranger, at this island now
The leaping light for your delight discovers,
Stand stable here

And silent be,
That through the channels of the ear
May wander like a river
The swaying sound of the sea.'

Having quit my job, I am now officially destined for France. A change of clothes fills my rucksack and I have a suitcase of books either written in French or that have a connection to France. They've been acquired, in the main, from charity shops and, after some investigation, I'm optimistic about selling at least two of them. *Tout l'inconnu de la Casbah* by Lucienne Favre was published in 1933 by the Baconnier Frères. Recounting life in Algier's Casbah, it is delicately illustrated by Charles Brouty, who also worked on other popular books concerning Algeria. The other banker is Norman Cameron's 1940s translation of Arthur Rimbaud's *A Season in Hell*, published by John Lehmann. Rimbaud himself published *Une Saison en Enfer*, an extended poem that later influenced the Surrealists.

The crossing is late at night on a ferry populated by as many staff as passengers. The crew, fresh and alert, crack jokes while the passengers, unused to the late hour, eat and drink in the canteen with an air of mournfulness. In between mouthfuls, I look out of the portholes. They aren't actually portholes as such, but I feel that the apertures, which are just big windows really, should carry more of a nautical connotation. It is dark outside and only with difficulty can I make out the movement of water. I think of school trips to France. Flick knives bought in Boulogne. Firecrackers too, and more interest shown in mopeds than boulangeries. On the ferry's return to Dover, a rumour spread fast that custom officials are as punitive as they are vigilant. In the ensuing panic, thirty contraband weapons were lost to the sea. Only Eddy had kept his nerve.

I drink an insipid cup of coffee (the last for some time, I imagine, since a quick return to England is not an option) before descending two decks to use up my English change on the fruit machines. Several passengers wanting French currency discover that the bureau de change is closed. Returning to the canteen, I feel strangely serene until approached by two sickly pale kids who brandish plastic toy guns. They make the inevitable sound effects before being ineffectually admonished by parents who look barely out of their teens. The only other person within range to be irritated is a fat man in smart business attire. He, however, seems to have set himself the task of exhausting the ship's entire supply of lager. Alcohol makes him oblivious to the noise or anyone else's company. I order a lager myself while it is still possible. Surveying the rest of the canteen, I wonder idly if there are any lone passengers of the opposite sex.

In French waters we reassemble with surprising efficiency and the coach leaves the ferry at Calais without a hitch. Shifting restlessly on hard seats, I try to trick myself into believing I am at ease. Some people evidently succeed, sleep carrying them away from the discomfort of the coach.

At 6.30 a.m. on an cold overcast morning in early October the coach reaches its Paris destination, a grotty bus station in the city's northern suburbs. In the bleakness that envelops the place and the moment, I experience a pang of self-pity. No family or friends clamour to meet me. The driver, a red faced man with beefy arms, opens up the belly of the coach and gets annoyed with the passengers impatient to reclaim their luggage. The removal of rucksacks and cases from the undercarriage is exclusively his preserve, even if it does involve a great deal of huffing and puffing.

The RER line quickly comes to my attention since it is situated on the other side of the car park. The vehicles are neatly aligned beneath a corrugated iron hangar. Little thought for environmental aesthetics, however, had gone into its construction. It quickly rids me of the naive notion that somehow everything in the City of Light is going to be of dazzling wonder.

If I'd managed to convince anyone to think of me as a non-tourist, my pointless act of deception abruptly ends at the ticket office. I ferret in a panicked mind for vaguely appropriate words to explain an undignified search for some change. Putting on my best apologetic face, I pull out a 100 franc note.

Misreading the metro map results in an ungainly stagger down the Champs Elysée. I regret my decision to stock up on some weighty classics of English literature in addition to the French books. Sweat burns at the edges of my eyes and I have an hour's wait before the tourist office opens. I sit down on the cold pavement and watch others gather outside the same building before we are all herded like cattle (the analogy embarrassingly apposite) into the building. Accommodation is everyone's natural priority. We queue to be told by blasé looking staff where a bed is to be found. A service is offered whereby hotels are telephoned to assess the likelihood of their having vacancies. The staff do not appreciate independent suggestions gleaned from Fodor's 'cost conscious' guide to Europe. The cheapest nightly rate that they come up with is 180 francs, which I agree to pay. The deal is fixed up and a map thrust into my hand with the hotel's location nonchalantly ringed in red ink. The hotel is close to the Basilica of the Sacred Heart in Montmartre. I want to declare: 'Hey I'm no tourist, this is a business trip.' I say nothing but leave with a spring in my step, seeing romance and adventure on the horizon.

Reality soon asserts itself. A soggy shower curtain is draped over the rim of a small bath. On the green linoleum floor there is a pool of water containing all the germs of the last occupant, whom I imagine suffers from unspeakably horrible diseases. The bathroom is windowless and the smell of dampness permeates into the bedroom. This consists of a creaky bed, a wardrobe and a chest of drawers. My belongings, transported in a navy blue rucksack, could fit into a single drawer but I leave them in the rucksack. I leave the suitcase unopened. The room looks out onto more insalubriousness. Clothes dangle from washing lines that criss-cross the gap between buildings. Brown rusted sheeting slopes down, from various levels, to meet in the square's middle. There are three soot-blackened stairways, clinging to the buildings' exterior, that seem to lead to nowhere.

The street into which I emerge smells bad. The stench of dog shit lingers. I look down at my shoes and see why. For 48 hours I haven't spoken to anyone in a non-official capacity. I need a beer, so enter a small bar to order one. The barman looks puzzled when I take my drink onto the terrace. The clouds have cleared and it's warm enough to sit outside. I sip at my drink while looking furtively at a skinny lady in chic garb on the adjoining table. Passers-by openly eye her up. Absorbed in a magazine, she doesn't seem to notice them. I get up and walk off with affected casualness. I walk for hours with no real aim in mind; picking up the smell of the Seine before glimpsing its waters.

119

The banks of the Seine are lined with green metal *bouquiniste* stalls. The bookselling tradition dates back to the seventeenth century when the Renaissance ushered in an era of 'vagabond' booksellers. They were to eventually set up fixed places of business alongside the river. I try to make conversation with one of them who isn't engrossed in a newspaper or book. Thwarted by my French, we both agree, with consoling smiles, to end our attempts at communication.

I wander into the city's Latin Quarter and then come across Gibert Jeune bookshop, a seven-storeyed bookshop on Boulevard Saint-Denis. What a p(a)lace. It is said to hold the biggest stock of books in France; providing literature for university students from all fields of study.

To help broach the subject of my French books, I buy the recently published French language edition of *A Prayer for Owen Meany* in the misguided belief that, knowing the story in English, it will help improve my language skills. An employee, a tiny man with large glasses and good English, expresses a modicum of interest in my business proposal. I arrange to bring the books in tomorrow. The rest of the day passes in a whirlwind of ideas and distractions. A rough calculation of my budgetary needs causes me to check into a hostel in the Marais district. It is cheaper than the previous hotel and has a friendlier receptionist.

Jacques is from a *pied noir* family, French nationals who were born in Algeria. Keen to practise his English, he listens as I tell him about my day and my bookselling intentions. It turns out that he spent some of his childhood in Oran and had relations who lived just outside Algiers. He asks me to bring down the book I have about the city. *(Tout l'inconnu de la Casbah by Lucienne Favre. Published in 1933, Baconnier frères Algier, 1933.)*

'You see the Casbah. It's so different. Not European,' he explains.

'In the Casbah no signs of colonisation. Narrow streets, so different. Beautiful.'

He continues to leaf interestedly though it. 'Look here.' Jacques mentions prostitutes; Favre comparing the indigenous women in a favourable light to their European counterparts whom he finds crude.

'I 'ave heard of Brouty, you know. He took Le Corbusier for walk around the Casbah. You know Le Corbusier?' I nod, not wishing to appear ignorant. And before I properly realise it, Jacques is negotiating a price. I ought to take the book first to Gibert Jeune but Jacques is insistent. 'I give 500 francs and three days 'ere for free,' he says.

'Three days?'

'And nights too, *biensûr*.'

'Four nights.'

We shake hands on the deal. Jacques is clearly delighted with his new purchase. Have I undersold? I console myself by thinking that his enthusiasm might have skewed his valuation of the book in the way that football fans might bet, regardless of the odds, on their team.

At Gibert Jeune the next day I end up showing my wares to a lady whose seniority, I gather, trumps the bespectacled small man when it comes to the buying of stock. After producing an assortment of paperbacks, I pull out the Rimbaud from my bag with a flourish. It doesn't create the impact I'd been hoping. Surprise is expressed at it having been translated at all. I point out the original black cloth with red plate and gold lettering on its spine. It has a colour frontispiece and six colour plates by

Keith Vaughan who has designed the dust jacket with distinctive free flowing lettering. Both the book and its dust jacket are in very good condition so I can't understand her muted response.

She doesn't even deign to make an offer, gesturing instead towards a glass bookcase used to display Gibert Jeune's *'livres a collectioner.'* I spot the familiar olive-green of Olympia's *Traveller's Companion.* It's William Burrough's *The Naked Lunch* which she takes out to show me the author's signature. I don't understand. Is it that they don't want translations of French works of literature. I accept an offer of 350 francs for the paperbacks and leave the shop with the Rimbaud.

Maybe it will get a better reception at Shakespeare and Co.

Foxford, Ireland, 1988

A flowing veil of weeds delays its removal. The falls, a riot of motion in rock and water some ninety yards downstream of Foxford's ancient bridge. Simon eventually fishes it out and prises it open to find that the old tin is watertight. Seeping out is the aroma of stale cigar while fresh light yields an iridescent splash of colour; the feathers of the bronze mallard, the blue jay and the pheasant, some enwrought with gold and silver and all intricately woven onto hooks in deadly disguise.

The room's former occupants have left behind a packet of Silk Cut cigarettes, water-stained copies of *Trout and Salmon*, and a book. We laugh when we read its title. *A River Runs Through It* by Norman Maclean. It becomes one of my favourite novellas. It's about the Macleans, a Presbyterian family during early twentieth century Montana whose opinions of life are filtered through their passion for fly-fishing. The novella is presented from the point of view of older brother Norman who goes on one last fishing trip with his rowdy and troubled younger brother Paul in an attempt to help him get his life on track.

My friend Simon, Joyce aficionado and former colleague, is tutoring me in that art of catching brown trout from Irish rivers. In casting a cold eye upon waters he can read a river and take from it handsome trout and even the occasional salmon. It's good to have salmon on the menu for a change. Our bed and breakfast doubles as a bar and restaurant, doesn't offer the richest variety of food but the family who run the place can't be faulted on their hospitality. They commiserate with due solemnity on what are mostly unsuccessful expeditions on my part. And they are pleased to toast Simon's successes. His dark handsome face lights up and he lets rip with his gift of the gab. Pints of Guinness are poured in celebration and in mock consolation. I don't really care. I'm much more troubled by a dilemma of affection.

I like being on the riverbank, lost in the Moy's mud and mysteries. I put down the rod to take it in. It's another country, obviously so but it is more than that. The peal of bells for mass; the shadows of owls flitting across the belfry and silhouettes of bats. Simon catches one in his line, extricating it gently before trudging upriver. I'm fishing with a jungle cock fly, intrigued by its design even if the trout don't appear to share my interest. Like a hallucination, Mary appears; her face ghostly pale in the moon's light. She scrambles down the bank.

'Any joy?'

A shake of the head. She follows a while and I want to embrace this girl whose mellifluous voice stirs the blood. 'See you another time, take care.'

'Bye.' I curse myself.

Train to Liverpool, 2006

Last time I got my camper van stuck in the entrance to a car park, so today I'm taking the train. It's a pleasant journey from Bangor; the mountains to the right, the sea to the left if you sit facing in the direction of travel. Before we arrive at Chester, a large ship, seemingly marooned on the sands, catches the eye. After noting its name as the *Duke of Lancaster*, I discover that it has its own appreciation society. And from their website I learn that: 'in 1979, as a former Sealink passenger ferry, it was beached in North Wales with the intention of turning it into a floating leisure and retail complex. The project never seemed to get off the ground and as such the ship has been on the banks of the River Dee.'

It transpires that the *Duke of Lancaster* was one of finest vessels afloat in the late fifties and early sixties. The first class quarters were the best around, silver service restaurants, state-rooms and luxurious cabins. The River Dee is tidal, and seeing the sandbanks and the ship, Shelley's poem comes to mind.

> '"My name is Ozymandias, king of kings:
> Look on my works, ye Mighty, and despair!"
> Nothing beside remains. Round the decay
> Of that colossal wreck, boundless and bare
> The lone and level sands stretch far away.'

In Henry Bohn's big bookshop in Liverpool I feel strangely lacklustre. There is plenty to interest the reader, collector and dealer alike. But I'm struggling to muster enthusiasm for the search. I wonder if the *Duke of Lancaster* is to blame. I leave the shop only with a handful of out of print paperbacks. But I also learn that the 12-volume Pilgrim set of Dickens' letters on display in the shop's window was offered by The Folio Society to its members for a knock down price of £400. I have a set in similarly good condition.

The trip hasn't been a wasted one since I return to Bangor with a typically eclectic range of titles from News from Nowhere, Liverpool's radical and community bookshop. They have something of an underrated second-hand section.

Porthmadog, 2005

As well as visiting a shop specialising in antique weaponry, I like going to Porthmadog for its sprawling junkshop/scrap yard in the back streets. They don't make many like this any more. You half expect the characters from *Steptoe and Son* to appear, only they'd be speaking in Welsh. To get to the books at the back I have to clamber over fridges, televisions and ironing boards. I rather enjoy doing so. The corrugated metal roof leaks in places but most of the books are unscathed.

Beneath a pile of Haynes car manuals, I find a collection of Rupert the Bear annuals from the seventies. They aren't old enough to command any real monetary value.

A man, smelling of milk who presides over the place, is surprised that I don't want them but consoled by my purchase of a book on the Tea Clipper ships.

I return to Bangor via Beddgelert. Much of the landscape in the Rupert stories is inspired by the local landscape of Snowdonia, notably around Beddgelert, where Alfred Bestall's family had a cottage. The character was created by the English artist Mary Tourtel and first appeared in the *Daily*

Express in 1920. In 1935 the mantle of Rupert artist and storyteller was taken over by Bestall, who was previously an illustrator for *Punch*.

Plotting with Shakespeare's Ghost in Tylers Bookshop, Bangor, 2005

Dan and I spend hours discussing his various options. He wants to keep his shop going but needs to dissolve a business partnership with someone who takes little active role in the day-to-day running of the shop. I want to help extend the used books section, which Dan thinks is a good idea, but if he breaks ties with his partner, the landlord can hike up the rent. We call it the Rubik cube of quandary; iron out one and another crops up. We scheme and plot, rather appropriately given the shop's history and its close proximity to Bangor's Cathedral. Local historians believe the shop to have once been the archdeacon's house, as mentioned in Henry IV Part I, which was the set Shakespeare play in my fifth form.

Act 3, Scene 1: Bangor. The archdeacon's house. The men take out a large map of Britain and divide it up as they have earlier discussed: after they defeat King Henry, Glyndŵr will get the western part of Britain – western England and all of Wales; Mortimer will get the south-east part of England, including London; Hotspur will get the northern part, home to his family.

Could Shakespeare have travelled here in the missing years? The building supports a stone chimneystack that fits the Tudor period. Glyndŵr is portrayed in Shakespeare's play

Henry IV, Part 1 (as Owen Glendower) as a wild and exotic man ruled by magic and emotion. Historians describe him as a charismatic leader. And there is possibly a connection to real history too. 'During Owain Glyndwr's rebellion, his delegates cloistered in secret session at Bangor with the envoys of his English fellow conspirators, Mortimer and the Earl of Northumberland, to divide the whole of the English realm between them. (from *The Matter of Wales* by Jan Morris).

Dan is great with the public and loves books. He doesn't seem to covet personal wealth, an attractive trait in a person but puzzling to those that harbour more commercial ambition. A customer thinks Dan is missing a trick by not advertising Tylers' historical credentials; using the bard and Glyndŵr as a ploy to pull in the tourists. I think Dan can go further still, it being likely that Thomas De Quincy passed by the shop during his wanderings in North Wales. He even took lodging in a 'small neat home' in Bangor; his landlady having been a servant in the family of Bishop of Bangor. In *Confessions of an English Opium Eater*, I hazily recall De Quincy's praise for Bangor's cemetery but I haven't been able to find this passage again in the book. Did I dream it?

Leaving 44 rue de l'Université, 1998

I am on the phone to Eddy, moaning. In the morning, there's a Mary Celeste feel to the place. Afternoons at least bring in more punters. I estimate that 75 per cent of the books are sold after 3 p.m. 'Why not open the shop then?' Eddy suggests. I laugh, tempted and Eddy goes on: 'They say the Christmas period for Harrods represents 70 per cent of its annual turnover. Maybe they should open only for those few weeks. You might start a revolution in the retail trade.'

It might be the routine, but the shop is now energy sapping; I'm reading less too. I start to covet customers' occupations, which is always a bad sign. I meet an Englishman who assembles cranes for a living in Southern France. As if erecting towering structures of metal was not difficult enough, he's chosen to exercise his trade over here. My first thoughts are of how he managed to acquire the scores of certificates that French bureaucracy would demand. By good fortune, it turns out he met an employer prepared to take his word on previous assignments and a joint effort was made to translate the relevant qualifications. Crane assembling isn't the sort of job in which you can easily bluff it as an experienced hand. He leaves the shop with a copy of *Jonathan Livingston Seagull*.

The itinerant bookseller John Edwards turns up, with his adorable dog, in his big red transit van. He's come from selling Wordsworth Classics and remainders to shops in Paris. In comparison, he sells little to me but doesn't take umbrage at the paucity of my orders. After a cup of tea and chat, he sets off for Barcelona, anticipating a swim en route in the sea at Sète. It's enough to bring on a strong dose of wanderlust.

It's no contest; football wins over shop management. I'm on the road, albeit until England are knocked out. A friend, working as a translator for the England Supporters Club, has got me complimentary tickets for all of England's World Cup matches. There are vast swathes of England shirts, bands playing the *Great Escape* theme tune and thousands of supporters milling about the stadiums without tickets; their dedication humbling. The games go by in a blur: a Scholes cracker in Marseille, disappointment in Toulouse (no second-hand bookshops either), more hurt in Saint Etienne. Thousands make do with TVs in the French bars in order to witness Owen's legendary goal before the inevitable let down. I return to Montpellier, deflated and once more shop bound.

There is, however, an escape route, one that biker Pete has helped to provide. Thanks to this maverick software designer, I am given an early introduction to the web's book selling potential. Receiving the first order (for a 1938 Penguin *Gulliver's Travels* illustrated throughout with wood-engravings by Theodore Naish) from my website was akin to an epiphany of sorts; I could trade without a retail premises in bricks and mortar.

The geography of the road was against us all along. Even friends have confessed that they can't face climbing the hill into the city's centre. And the promise of human traffic from the new tram stop proves illusory. With heavy hearts and an unacknowledged relief, we close the shop, placing a sign in the window: 'Words failed me.'

Catalogue Gazing, Bangor, 2009

For O-Level we studied *Lord of the Flies* whose author, William Golding, had taught our English teacher, and I used to wonder if Mr Whiteside was privy to the allegorical novel's finer interpretations. Whenever the book comes up at auctions, as one did last year at the Dominic Winters Auction House near Cirencester, I do a double take. I was, though, and remain more appreciative of *The Adventures of Huckleberry Finn*, the other major work of literature that Mr Whiteside selected for study. Especially that revelatory passage when Huck rejects the advice of his 'conscience', which continues to tell him that in helping Jim escape to freedom, he is stealing Miss Watson's property. Telling himself 'All right, then, I'll go to hell!', Huck, listening to a deeper 'conscience', resolves to free Jim.

I am gazing at a first edition of this book, or rather a photograph of it in the pages of a Dominic Winter Catalogue for an auction in 2008. The book is bound in green cloth which bears a picture of Huck on the cover, standing in a field of corn, blocked in gold. *(1st American Edition, mixed issue, Charles L. Webster, New York, 1885, wood eng. frontis and numerous letterpress vigns., heliotype port. title-page with copyright notice on verso dated 1884, occn. creasing to corners, and pp. 163/4 with piece missing from upper outer blank corner, some light soiling, modern bookplate, orig. pictorial green cloth gilt, spine ends frayed with sl. loss, corners showing, 8vo)*

I try to interpret what the book's image in the catalogue means to me. It's a false dichotomy; the book as a physical object and the story within. For they become intertwined. Mark Twain's book, commonly recognised as one of the great American novels, inspired us to 'play hookey' and smoke cigars on the banks of the Thames. But more importantly it made us realise that stories are not the possession of any elite. When it came to respective social backgrounds, I was Tom to Eddy's Huck. Eddy said recently himself that for his mother 'scrawling a note to the milkman was breaking new literary ground'.

From the photograph in the catalogue you can clearly make out the novel's title. Bundles of sticks, also blocked in gold, depict the first letters of Huckleberry Finn's name, H and F. And the full title is *Adventures of Huckleberry Finn (Tom Sawyer's Comrade)*. Upon completion, the novel's title closely paralleled its predecessor's. Unlike *The Adventures of Tom*

Sawyer, Twain's *Adventures of Huckleberry Finn* does not have the definite article as a part of its proper title. Essayist and critic Philip Young states that this absence represents the 'never fulfilled anticipations' of Huck's adventures – while Tom's adventures were completed by the end of his novel, Huck's narrative ends with his stated intention to head West.

If I had £3000 to spare, I'd be tempted to invest in such a book. Not that it's the pinnacle for Mark Twain (Samuel Langhorne Clemens) collectors. *A blue cloth edition, which is more scarce than the green cloth edition, was issued in a smaller quantity. A three-quarter morocco leather edition was also issued. It is extremely scarce. There were only five hundred of the leather bound copies issued.*

Paris 1991, Second Stint

The bank is expressing its mounting frustration in the letters sent to my parents' address.

Unwittingly, I have discovered that an overdrawn account cannot prevent the holder from cashing in travellers' cheques, regardless of when they were issued. I have used the money to pay two months' rent in advance. Delgado insisted.

This enigmatic Spaniard is sub-letting only the bedroom of a council flat on the seventh floor of a tower block near Belleville. The flat has little going for it except for a wonderful view of the Eiffel Tower. The sitting room is Delgado's living quarters. Not that he lives here much. He's out all day, returning only late at night to the flat before rising early to beat me out in the mornings. Despite making rare appearances, Delgado is obsessed by the flat's appearance and isn't impressed when Eddy stays over. Empty beer cans and uncleaned ashtrays leave him foul tempered for days and I'm very much in his bad books after last Saturday night. The lock jammed in the toilet door with me on the wrong side. Luckily, Eddy was in the flat and the fire brigade could be called to rescue me. An axe produced a gaping hole in the door where the lock had once been and I was able to emerge with profuse gratitude. '*Merci millefois. Voulez vous une tasse du thé.*' The firemen decline politely and wonder what the hell are two English lads doing in an HLM flat in the eastern suburbs of Paris. The captain made a cursory request for our IDs before leaving. Delgado still will not accept an apology or my explanation of what happened. He is, for once, spending Saturday morning in his room. So I take to the streets even though I'm not meeting up with Eddy and his girlfriend for several hours.

I wander along the Seine's embankments, checking out the *bouquinists*. Anatole France knew of 'no sweeter, gentler pleasure than to go a book hunting' here. I have two travellers' cheques left but these are for real emergencies. The overdraft does register on my conscience though, and so effectively prevents me from serious perusal. And I don't need anything else to read. Phil has lent me a book written by Joris-Karl Huysmans called *A Rebours* which is translated into English as *Against Nature*.

A wildly original *fin-de-siècle* novel, *Against Nature* follows its sole character, Des Esseintes, an aristocrat who retreats to an isolated villa where he indulges his taste for luxury and excess. The book exhibits anxiety about preserving a sense of self in the face of cultural change. To combat this anxiety, the decadent hero of the novel embraces a melancholic identity. I have developed a sneaking regard for Des Esseintes who is very much a book obsessive. 'Des Esseintes was morbid devotee of the unique, and he was rich enough to print his favourite books in editions of one copy. He had Poe's *Arthur Gordon Pym* thus specially printed for him on pure linen-laid paper, hand picked, bearing a sea-gull for water mark, and bound in sea-green morocco; his copy of the Diaboliques of Barbeyd'Aurvilly was specially printed for him on an authentic vellum blessed by the Church.'

I go in search of his creator and find rue Suger where he lived, and a confirmatory plaque: *Ici est né, le 5 février 1848, J.-K. HUYSMANS, Ecrivain français.*

Later, he had a road in the sixth arrondissement in Paris named after him. My legs feel tired and I become aware of the time. From starting out hours in advance, I now risk turning up late. Eddy won't mind but Sylvia might.

Eddy met Sylvia at the language school where they both now work. Sylvia started to teach English as a foreign language after an aborted career in marine biology. In Thailand, she'd worked on prawn farms but, overnight, the bottom fell out of that market when the Japanese Emperor Hirohito died; his people forsaking the crustaceans as a mark of respect.

Today I'm introducing them to an oasis of peace in this busy city, intending to drag them around the Cimetière du Père-Lachaise. Statues, tombstones and crypts dominate the landscape but also lend a romantic atmosphere to the cobbled avenues that run amid trees on the uneven ground. Ostentatiousness abounds but there remains something affecting in these funeral monuments, many of which are in an advanced state of dilapidation. Eddy and Sylvia, upon arriving, both agree. Below is what Flaubert thought:

'The tombs stood among the trees: broken columns, pyramids, temples, dolmens, obelisks, and Etruscan vaults with doors of bronze. In some of them might be seen funereal boudoirs, so to speak, with rustic arm-chairs and folding-stools. Spiders' webs hung like rags from the little chains of the urns; and the bouquets of satin ribbons and the crucifixes were covered with dust. Everywhere, between the balusters on the tombstones, were crowns of immortals and chandeliers, vases, flowers, black discs set off with gold letters, and plaster statuettes of little boys or little girls or angels suspended in the air by brass wires; several of them having even a roof of zinc overhead.'

Famous people are buried here including Musset, Chopin, Molière, Modigliani, Balzac, Colette, Oscar Wilde, Delacroix, Balzac and Jim Morrison in whom Sylvia, being a Doors fan, has expressed interest. A local florist sells us a leaflet that is unashamedly a map of the famous dead with co-ordinates of where to find their tombs, e.g. *Edith Piaf Chanteuse 97 e Div n-4*.

Some visitors to the cemetery are ticking off the names like seasoned gravestone hunters. Simone Signoret's grave is conspicuously festooned with flowers. We seek out Oscar Wilde's tomb; a sphinx-inspired angel sculpted by Jacob Epstein. On one side of the memorial are tributes to Wilde's art and achievements. Cited is Oxford's esteemed Classics prize and his epitaph is a quote from *The Ballad of Reading Gaol*:

'And alien tears will fill for him
Pity's long broken urn,

For his mourners will be outcast men,
And outcasts always mourn.'

The monument is covered with lipstick kisses. Would Wildean gifts of lyricism be imparted to the kisser like the legend of the Blarney Stone? Kiss the stone of eloquence and you'll never again be lost for words.

Sylvia is impatient to get going. Arrows chalked on gravestones point the way to the Morrison mourners. A German youth is drinking beer while listening to *The River* on his cassette player. A stout Australian woman is translating the lyrics of the same song for the benefit of a French schoolboy. A group of hippie girls with long, unkempt hair sit around a Primus stove boiling water to make tea. There are a few punks and the denim jacket brigade is also represented. A man sporting a hat of green feathers obscures Morrison's actual grave, it being of modest proportions. He moves and we can then read: JAMES DOUGLAS MORRISON 1943–1977 ΚΑΤΑ ΤΟΩΠ ΔΛΦΜΩΜΛ ΞΛΨΤΩΨ (Greek with a multitude of interpretations (To the divine spirit within himself, He caused his own demons, True to his own spirit).

In front of the grave are three joints; cannabis deemed more appropriate than a bouquet of flowers. We loiter, not knowing quite what is expected of us. Some people stoop to partake in a ceremonial toke before quickly extinguishing the joint or passing it on with an embarrassed air. Death has failed to grant Jim Morrison the anonymity he was said to have craved; an escape from idolatry. Eddy is disconcerted to see that most tombstones within a ten metre radius of Jim Morrison's are covered in graffiti, much of it being The Doors' lyrics. Sylvia and I also question this spray can adulation. In

135

making their shrine to Jim Morrison, the mourners have desecrated the tombs of others.

After several weeks of unemployment, I became maniacally jealous of other people engaged in ordinary and seemingly mundane activities. Couriers, roadside labourers, just about anyone having a job upon which to focus. I look forward with exaggerated relish to dish-washing in Montparnasse. The night before I'm due to start, I cash a travellers' cheque in spite of Eddy's protestations.

He and I are both in drunken awe of La Notre Dame which, viewed from Le Pont Tourbelle, appears to me as a huge, deformed heart, the exterior of the apse bursting out with arteries. Earlier in the evening we attended a book signing in the Village Voice bookshop. We went along to listen to Don DeLillo's pre-signing spiel about *Mao II* which is his tenth novel. His intellectual earnestness made an impression on us. But now all we can recall is the sentence: 'The future belongs to crowds.' After the talk we crawled into and out of various Irish pubs, finishing up in The Oscar Wilde. In the years to come, will Parisians be drinking in The Seamus Heaney? The alcohol makes Eddy maudlin. He is a little fed up with the teaching. I empathise, remembering Madrid when I sometimes felt like an impostor, asking colleagues what a gerund was. My experiences weren't like anything out of *The Education Of Hyman Kaplan*. 'I've got to get out before we started on the past perfect continuous,' declares Eddy.

Irish pubs and Breton creperies; one chain importing Guinness with bonhomie while the other specialises in cider with Breton dairy products. There are, however, similarities: the franchised decor of uniformity and the businesses' lucrativeness.

I have no difficulty in locating 'Mont St Michel' in Montparnasse. At 11.15 a.m., as arranged, I walk into the creperie and make for the bar, squeezing myself past tables and chairs. Up from behind the bar pops the smiling face of a man with a viciously receding hairline. His expansive smile conveys the warmest of greeting. But before either of us can speak, an emaciated individual appears with a cigarette poking out of his sullen face.

'Luc?' I ask. He nods and makes it obvious I am expected to follow as he descends a spiral staircase. The cavernous cellar turns out to be the kitchen and where the restaurant's dishes are cleaned.

On trolleys and shelves is piled a mountain range of food-stained plates. Stack upon stack of crockery. There are also smaller piles of white bowls on a table amid the cutlery and glasses that bear the remnants of last night's wine and cider. Luc doesn't trouble himself to speak – perhaps distrustful of my French. Body language is used to explain what is required. A preliminary clean to remove most of the food and the cigarettes butts; a knife used to scrape the debris into a bin liner. The plates are then to be placed (with loving care if his gesture, made in slow motion, is anything to go by) into an industrial cleaner. A green button is pressed and the machine makes a rumbling sound for the three minutes it functions on a timer. Hey presto. The plates are removed in a puff of steam to be neatly stacked on a trolley.

Luc leaves without a word and I surmise that I am to get on with it. The cable operating the dumb waiter makes a creaking noise under the strain. A stockily built Indian about my age is filling it with crates of Perrier. Having sent it heavenwards into the eating arena he comes over and is delighted to find that I'm English. 'It good job. Easy work,' he says. He wants to talk but has to react to instructions that are being barked down the intercom. More cider needed. Singh complies before efficiently preparing the salads.

After several hours of tedium, I can just about see the end in sight but then Singh carries over more plates from the lunchtime service.

We eventually emerge from the kitchen. The boss isn't about so Santos, who is Portuguese, can speak freely behind the counter. 'Engine off,' he says before treating us each to a fabulous banana and chocolate crepe.

Another man in his forties turns out to be the real boss. Singh explains that that he owns four creperies in the district, two in the same road. Luc is second in command.

After eating, I get ready to leave. Singh will hang around as he also works the night shift. He matter-of-factly tells me that afterwards he'll visit a brothel. 'I've been going there for three years.' Five minutes earlier he had been describing to me the beauty of the *Mahabharata*, a celebrated and sacred epic poem of the Hindus, written in Sanskrit.

Days pass. Dishes are washed. In the bowels of the creperie, I try to calculate how many dishes I've washed in my lifetime, my current job boosting significantly my daily average. I imagine a dishwashing day of reckoning whereby a mighty column of plates reaches high like Jacob's ladder into the clouds of God's kingdom.

My French is improving but the result is a chipping away at illusions I'd naively held onto until recent weeks. People the world over wallow verbally in the mundane routine of everyday life and that the weather is chief among their preoccupations.

Mornings drag by, after which I play exuberant games of football with ex pats in the Jardin des Tuileries. Eddy plays too and it's the only time we now spend together. Eddy has moved in with Sylvia and it's weeks since I saw Delgado. I spend most evenings with a book for company. I am re-reading Edgar Allan Poe's only complete novel, *The Narrative of Arthur Gordon Pym of Nantucket*.

> 'Having barely escaped this danger, our attention was now directed to the dreadful imminency of another – that of absolute starvation for we found the whole bottom, from within two or three feet of the bends as far as the keel, together with the keel itself, thickly covered with large barnacles, which proved to be excellent and highly nutritious food.'

I keep this book close to my bed as a talismanic object, hoping to use it to draw upon some of mankind's innate resourcefulness. Pym's salvation lay, unknown, just yards beneath his feet. Maybe mine is similarly within reach, requiring just a mere helping nudge of fate.

Shakespeare, Avignon, 1994

Author, former harpsichord maker, environmental activist, Wolfgang Zuckermann, now in his seventies, has recently opened a bookshop in Avignon. He's named it Shakespeare in honour of Sylvia Beach's original Shakespeare & Co. opened in Paris in 1919.

Having opened our bookshops at roughly the same time, we like to compare experiences and even our respective takings. He kindly listens to my complaints over *'les charges sociales'*. Wolfgang has astutely set up his shop as an association to avoid such costs. I call it wisdom.

Fulham Broadway, 1987

'Just another Saturday. Chelsea v Arsenal 1–0. Everybody went to Chelsea on Saturday to continue the party, and it lasted for another fifteen minutes, until something – a Hayes miss, or a Caesar back-pass, I can't remember now – provoked the howls of frustration and irritation that you could have heard on any Saturday of the previous years.' From *Fever Pitch, A Fan's Life* by Nick Hornby.

I went to this game but, being a Chelsea fan, experienced rather different emotions on the day. I wouldn't have expected Nick Hornby to appreciate the fragile artistry of Pat Nevin or the surging runs of David Speedie. As home supporters, we are first to stream out from the ground. Outside I catch that smell of league football; the mingling odours of cigarettes, hotdogs and horse manure. The crowd is mostly good-natured, buoyed by unexpected victory, but there are still men who proceed down the Kings Road with an air of menace about them.

I check out a nearby second-hand bookstall. The exhilaration of the game is beginning to fade, replaced by a warm glow of satisfaction, but my mind can't focus in the search for books. Random stupid thoughts assail me; given his career as gunrunner, would Rimbaud have been an Arsenal fan? The Arsenal hordes will soon be let out. I don't intend to loiter. There are old match progammes but I've never been really tempted by these. Like memories, they are somehow infinite and yet ephemeral.

My loyalty to the club dates to junior school when teachers generally held less liberal and caring attitudes towards children from rough neighbourhoods.

Eddy makes a resplendent entrance into the classroom, flouting school dress convention. The form teacher, Mrs Bremner, affectedly holds her mouth wide open as Eddy shuffles self-consciously past her, a striking blue figure amidst a room filling with its daily complement of grey jumpers. Eddy drops behind an ink-scrawled desk and into a chair also given the full graffiti treatment. But his swift movements fail to conceal the football kit. Aside from white socks and white stripes running down the sides of his shorts, Eddy is clad in cotton dyed blue in sporting allegiance. Mrs Bremner makes certain that her expression of shock has been universally perceived before she speaks.

What I find distracting is the eerie inertness of Eddy's head and his thick messy hair. From my angle his head is barely eclipsed by the silver strands on the head of his inquisitor. For a moment I have a ridiculous impression they are kissing. The threat of banishment is stridently issued in tones that belie Mrs Bremner's short and rather peculiar stature. A huge pair of breasts induces a stoop in her posture, and her pupils, keen to pay testimony to their cruel wit, brand her as the 'milk float', a nickname that proves durable.

Eddy looks unruffled. Maybe it's shock. But from this moment I know that I'm a Chelsea boy too.

Bangor, January 2010

In one of the Sillitoe boxes, I might have discovered a story about a man with confused ambitions who must resist a tendency to fixate on limited editions (even his washing machine is a first edition Hotpoint). Amid tales of travel, written in the present tense because that is how he lives them, are chance meetings with verse and prose. He puzzles over the reliability of memory. Is it a present representation of the past? Or the actual past, laid down in neural pathways, resurfacing in the present? It would seem difficult to filter out all the fiction from the fact. Whatever memories are, writing about them is an attempt to impose if not an order then at least some sort of theme to a life lacking in clear direction. Amid a stream of consciousness, he recollects: The births of his children. The polished syntax of a Penguin rep. A knife point mugging in Barcelona. Finding B. S. Johnson's *Trawl* in a box of Mills and Boon. Diarrhoea on a Corfu beach. Samuel Beckett's miniature signature. The pallor on the face of a young waitress behind a fish and chips counter. Led Zep taking to the Knebworth stage. Hell's Angels on a Devon beach. MacGowan mud pelting at Glastonbury. Watching *Match of the Day* in a post-operation painkiller high. Drinking tea with an Israeli soldier beside Bala lake. Finding reminder notes in a hymnbook that belonged to a church organist, recently deceased. A hashish bean soup in Corsica. Impromptu kick abouts.

Life, at times, has an overwhelming intensity. The exhilaration may cause dizziness, and he self-prescribes autonomy to loaf about in imagined worlds, to deal in books and to dream. A buzz of expectation to banish the banal. Groping among the dirt and dust at the bottom of boxes, fingers eager to uncover rare, limited editions, he can lose himself 'so that time and place and circumstances are annihilated in this sweet game, as in no other sport'. There is always the chance of a bargain, whether it be found in the shelves at Any Amount of Books in Charing Cross Road or from Pwllheli public library offloading old stock. He must learn, however, to abstain from snapping up books that were once bargains. The internet plays merry havoc with prices. The perennial fear of dealers, that the rare books will die out, is perhaps a more justified one these days. Charity shops have got savvy. Auctions generally are a better bet. Delving into a box bought at a recent sale, with the beetles and spiders scuttling away, he discovers two books that, being hidden beneath old newspapers, had escaped everybody's attention. One book, with colour plates that illustrate beautifully the varieties of pheasants, will pay for a flight to Mumbai.

And the other is a book with a passage in it that made a strong impression on him several decades ago, *A Sentimental Education* by Gustave Flaubert. In it somewhere is an acceptance by Frederic Moreau, the novel's protagonist, of life's vicissitudes, a useful if rather bland philosophy. He rereads the novel but fails to locate the passage. Is it another figment of his imagination? Maybe it's to be found in *Madame Bovary*, a more famous work of literature, perhaps, with memorable imagery.

'Whereas the truth is that fullness of soul can sometimes overflow in utter vapidity of language, for none of us can express the exact measure of his needs or his thoughts or his sorrows; and human speech is like a cracked kettle on which we tap crude rhythms for bears to dance to, while we long to make music that will melt the stars.'

He continues to hunt with delusions of grandeur; to stumble upon an 'Et Tu Healy', a broadsheet poem by James Joyce said to have been published when Joyce was nine years old. Or better still; a *'Love's Labors Won,'* a Shakespeare lost play achieving mythical status since 1953, when Solomon Pottesman discovered it in the 1603 booklist of the stationer Christopher Hunt, listed as printed in quarto: 'Marchant Of Vennis, Taming Of A Shrew, Loves Labour Lost, Loves Labour Won.'

The story ends before an aborted enquiry into the ethics of selling them, for as Percy Fitzgerald in the *Book Fancier* says: 'the loyal heart would feel a twinge or scruple, as he carries off from the humble and ignorant dealer, for a shilling or two, a volume that may be worth ten or twelve pounds. No sophistry, he concludes, will veil the sharpness of transaction, in which profit is made of poverty and ignorance.' This applies to capitalism itself but the realisation of it does not deter the story's protagonist, now middle aged, from planning more journeys, exploratory missions to the East whereby en route he may even seek some Vedantic wisdom. Beside his bed is a well-thumbed copy of the *Let's Go Guide to India* with the addresses of Delhi's bookshops underlined. He continues to chase after it, still searching.

PARTHIAN

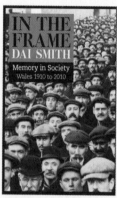

IN THE FRAME
DAI SMITH
Memory in Society
Wales 1910 to 2010

"... HIS APPROACH IS THOROUGH AND
HIS EXCITEMENT CONTAGIOUS ..."
the Independent on Sunday

CLOUD ROAD:
A Journey Through the Inca Heartland

JOHN HARRISON

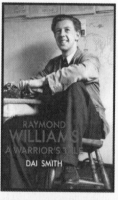

RAYMOND
WILLIAMS
A WARRIOR'S TALE
DAI SMITH

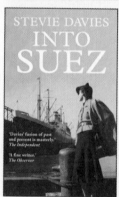

STEVIE DAVIES
INTO
SUEZ

'Davies' fusion of past
and present is masterly.'
The Independent

'A fine writer.'
The Observer

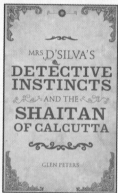

MRS D'SILVA'S
DETECTIVE
INSTINCTS
AND THE
SHAITAN
OF CALCUTTA

GLEN PETERS

NIALL GRIFFITHS
TEN POUND POM

"NIALL GRIFFITHS IS AN ACTUAL LITERARY STAR."
DAILY TELEGRAPH

www.parthianbooks.com